UNION CASTLE

-THE FORGOTTEN NAVY

Peter Abbott

an avid publication

UNION CASTLE
-THE FORGOTTEN NAVY
by
Peter Abbott

ISBN 1 902964 21 7

© Peter Abbott 2001

Front cover: SS *Kenya Castle* at Dar-es-Salaam in 1952.
Frontispiece : The first motor vessel in the Union-Castle fleet. RMMV *Carnarvon Castle*. Rear cover: Five advertising stamps used by the Union-Castle company in 1914.

Editing, Typeset and cover design by William David Roberts MA
Avid Publications. © 2001

Other Publications from Avid are listed at the rear of this book.

To Order Books or Videos Direct Contact:-
Avid Publications, Garth Boulevard, Hr. Bebington,
Wirral, Merseyside, UK. CH63 5LS.
Tel / Fax (44) 0151 645 2047
Look at the books and videos via the internet on
http://www.avidpublications.co.uk
E-mail info@avidpublications.co.uk

CONTENTS

The Author

Peter Abbott joined the Union-Castle Line in April 1951. He became a Purser's Clerk and his first ship was the *Bloemfontein Castle.* He served on a number of the Company's ships in his career at sea; most of the time on the Round Africa run, during a period when great changes were beginning to take place in all of the African Colonies.

After leaving the sea he became a college lecturer and upon retirement he and he wife Sue lived in Cape Town for a number of years where much of the research for this book was done.

To my wife Sue

and my Granddaughter Sarah

INTRODUCTION

So much has been written about the Mail service to the Cape that the Union-Castle Line operated for 120 years, that it is easy to forget the other routes, some of which they pioneered over almost the same period of time.

The intermediate service was one that was very successful and survived for approaching a hundred years. Others were less so, being on occasion overtaken by events. The middle of the nineteenth century saw the growing interest of the European powers in Africa. The East coast of the continent was hardly known at all, let alone what lay behind the coastal strip. Half way through the century, things began to change. It was when Doctor Livingstone made the initial journey from the west coast to the east, that the so-called "Dark Continent" attracted massive public attention and interest, in Britain and elsewhere.

It was during the same period that shipping companies like Cunard, P. & O. and the Union Line, appeared on the scene. This was because of the development of the steam ship. Not only did services become more reliable, but also the time taken to reach India and other distant parts was considerably reduced. At this time there were still not many passengers travelling to Africa and the Far East. Few colonies had been established, but as more 'outposts' were established, so passenger numbers increased. At first, most passengers were soldiers, but this gradually changed to civil servants, clerks, engineers etc. together with their families. The Europeans who colonised the Cape and Natal were few in number, and the population was mostly based in the towns like Cape Town and Durban. In addition, there were many farms scattered in the hinterland. Earlier, in 1835, the Great Trek had commenced when more than 10,000 Boers left the Cape Colony and trekked across the Orange River, founding the Orange Free State and the Transvaal.

It was one thing though to be a First Class passenger on these early steamships. It was quite another thing to travel steerage. Even in the First Class conditions were hardly luxurious, with cabins that were no more than twelve feet square. Passengers had to supply their own furniture, which would be off loaded at their destination and then transported to their new home.

To travel steerage was not far removed from the slave trade. It was cheap, but in general, six feet square was the space shared by four people. Because of contaminated water, dysentery was common, and cholera regularly carried off a number of the steerage passengers. Improvements in standards did begin to take place at the beginning of the 1850's.

Only Portugal, France and Britain had any substantial colonial interests in Africa in 1850. The Portuguese were long established in Mozambique on the East Coast and Angola on the West. Britain was present on the West Coast and at the Cape, and France also was established on the West Coast. Even by 1880 only very limited areas of Africa had been colonised and in most cases it still remained the coastal fringe. However, by 1914, with the exception of Ethiopia and Liberia, the whole of Africa had been partitioned and colonised by the three countries already mentioned, together with Germany, Belgium, Spain and Italy.

As far as the East Coast was concerned, in the first half of the nineteenth century, the real power was wielded by the Omani's, led by the Sultan of Zanzibar. They had been established for several hundred years and, at that time, still controlled a considerable empire. They had first ruled from Muscat in Oman, before Sultan Seyyid Said moved to Zanzibar in 1832. At that point they controlled the East Coast from the Kenyan border in the North to the Tanzanian boundary in the South. The African interior may have been unknown to the Europeans, but the Arab slave traders had ventured far into the interior in search of ivory, both black and white. The black slaves were the main basis of the Omani power and wealth. There's an old Arab saying which sums up Zanzibar's situation, which translated reads as follows:

' When the flute is heard in Zanzibar,
All Africa east of the Lakes must dance. '

The Omani Empire at one time also stretched eastward as they controlled parts of the coast of what is now Pakistan. In earlier times they traded as far as China and Chinese junks were calling at the island of Zanzibar. The African wild animals, in particular the giraffe, fascinated the Chinese.

The main instrument of the Omani success was the dhow. There are many different types of dhow and these vessels are in direct descent from the sailing ships of ancient times, which first appeared on the seas of the Near East. The largest ocean going vessels were about two hundred tons with the smaller ones being used mainly in the coastal trade.

The early British explorers had all condemned the slave trade. Doctor Livingstone had said that it was the duty of Britain to put an end to the trade in East Africa. In fact Britain had been in the forefront, since the latter part of the eighteenth century, to stop the trade on the West Coast. Denmark was the first country to abolish slavery in 1804, followed by Britain three years later. Gradually more and more of the other powers followed suit. By the middle of the nineteenth century, British warships based on Simonstown in the Cape, were patrolling the seas off the East coast to try and capture the slave dhows. Successful seizures, together with their crews, were brought to Cape Town where their fate was decided by the Commission for the Suppression of the Slave Trade. In some cases the slaves were still on board when a dhow was captured and they also ended up in Simonstown.

Although the wholesale shipping of slaves to Oman and to Persia had been stopped by the activities of the British, this is not the end of the story. Once the

2

trade had been prohibited it had just gone underground and become more secretive. In the 1930's cases of slave trading and ownership continued and even recently, evidence of the owning of slaves in the Sudan has come to light. The abolition of slavery was not the reason the European Powers rushed in to divide Africa between them. The "Scramble for Africa", as it became known, was partly for national prestige, partly for political and economic expansion and ultimately for strategic reasons. Africa was important to Britain initially was because the only sea route to India was via the Cape. Trade was becoming all-important hence the growth of the major shipping companies at this time. An important event occurred in 1869 when the Suez Canal was opened. For some years the canal had little impact and the majority of ships still sailed round the Cape. The more perceptive could see clearly what an effect the canal would eventually have and the celebrations surrounding the opening were extravagant to say the least.

November 17th 1869 was the date fixed for the grand opening of the Canal. This was to be a magnificent fete to celebrate the event, which was considered to be one of the greatest engineering achievements of the Century. Every European Royal family would be represented and even Thomas Cook would be present, escorting a party of one hundred from Britain at fifty guineas a head. Altogether some six thousand guests were expected and food and suitable accommodation would have to be provided. Around five hundred cooks and a thousand servants were brought in from Italy and France.

It was a race against time to prepare everything and there were occasions when it looked as though the opening would have to be delayed, but when the day dawned and Empress Eugenie of France arrived, all was ready. However, word soon reached Port Said that an Egyptian frigate had gone aground in the canal and was completely blocking it. Attempts were made to remove the ship without any success. It was even contemplated that the vessel may have to be blown up. The time for the departure of the fleet arrived, and the ships, led by *L'Aigle* with the Empress and Ferdinand de Lesseps on board, entered the Canal. Five minutes before they were due to reach the frigate, word was received that the way was clear, much to the relief of everyone. When the *L'Aigle* reached Kantara, she passed the frigate, which fired a salute.

By early evening the procession of ships had arrived at Lake Timsah. There had been a few problems with ships grounding, but all but two had berthed by midnight. Meanwhile, one of the greatest parties of all time had started. There were fireworks in front of the Viceroy's Palace and huge dinner parties were taking place in marquees and tents. Altogether, between seven and eight thousand people sat down to a sumptuous dinner, which included vintage wines. After dinner dancers, jugglers and singers entertained the guests.

The following day some of the ships carried on to Suez, with others stopping for the night at the Bitter Lakes before completing the journey the next day.

Eighteen months after the ceremony, 486 ships with 26,875 passengers had passed through the canal. This was less than twenty-seven ships a month on average, which was far short of what had been anticipated. It was some time before the traffic reached the level where it became profitable. By 1871 the price of the shares in the Canal Company had fallen from 500 to 208 francs and it was to take several years before the price of the shares went back to near the issue price of 500 francs.

Nearly all the ships that used the Canal, were bound for India and the Far East. Trade was slow to develop to and from East Africa and was not helped by poor port facilities. Maritime trade began to increase when the Colonial powers began building railways. This provided cargoes in the form of track, sleepers, engines and rolling stock, followed later by large shipments of steam coal. The first railway to the interior was started in Lourenco Marques in 1887, followed by the line up country from Tanga, and another from Beira to the Rhodesias. In 1895 the line from Mombasa to Uganda via Nairobi was started and, in 1905, the Germans began the line from Dar-es-Salaam to the Lakes.

It was in 1857 that the Union Steam Ship Company came on the scene, when the Line won the mail contract for the Cape. This was only a beginning and it was not long before the Company was involved in the coastal trade as far as Durban. Also, because the mail service was only monthly, it became the practice to introduce additional intermediate sailings to the Cape, and the ships themselves soon came to be called "Intermediates". Within seven years a service to Mauritius had started and within a further ten, the vessels were sailing up the East coast as far as Zanzibar. With the expansion of British interests in what was first called British East Africa, there came new services to Mombasa and eventually the Round Africa run came into being.

CHAPTER 1 - THE EARLY YEARS *1854 - 1879*

The origins of the Union Line go back to 1853. By that time most of the ocean going steamships that were employed on the routes to India and the Far East were based in Southampton. Among the companies that were already becoming established were P. & O. and Royal Mail. With the increasing number of steamers using the port, the demand for bunker coal was rising. This brought about the formation of a steam collier business called the Southampton Steam Shipping Company. The name was changed within days when the Company was registered, to the Union Steam Collier Company. The intention of the directors was to build five steamships, which would be used to transport coal from South Wales to Southampton.

In 1853 war had broken out between Turkey and Russia and although at that time they were not involved in the conflict, both British and French warships were soon operating in the Black Sea. By March 1854, Great Britain had become involved as well as France, on the side of Turkey and was at war with Russia. Even before the involvement of Britain in the conflict merchant ships were being commandeered by the Government to transport both troops and supplies to the war zone.

By June 1854 the steamship *Union*, the first of the Company's ships to be completed, was busy transporting 500 tons of coal per voyage from Cardiff to Southampton. By 1855 the other four ships, namely the *Briton, Saxon, Norman* and *Dane* had all come in to service. The P. & O. Company was at the time operating the Levant Line to Turkey and Malta. It was not long though before the government chartered their ships for the Crimea campaign. The Union Company then took over the Levant service, sailing principally to Constantinople and Smyrna. This did not last long, as the Union Line ships were also taken over by the government and almost immediately all five of the Union Line ships were gainfully employed and the Company was doing very well. So much so that another ship was purchased and named *Celt*.

With the defeat of Russia in 1856 the war in the Crimea was over and the ships returned to their normal trade. However, because of the war, large stocks of coal had built up at Southampton so that the Union ships were not required for this purpose. The Company then decided to enter the general cargo trade and therefore changed the name of the Line to the Union Steam Ship Company Limited. First of all in September 1856 they started a service to Brazil, but this was not successful and neither was an alternative venture to Hamburg. By 1857 the Line was chartering its ships to other companies, and it was at this point that they tendered for the Cape Mail contract and were successful in winning it.

The first mail ship, the *Dane,* sailed from Southampton on the 15th September 1857 to inaugurate a service that was to last for one hundred and twenty years. *Dane* arrived in Table Bay forty-four days later where she joined more than sixty ships that were already anchored in the Bay. This large number of vessels was due to the mutiny in India that was taking place at the time. While the *Dane* was there the fleet was joined by the two largest ships in the world. The first of these was Brunel's *Great Britain* and the second was the *Himalaya,* which was a trooper having previously carried soldiers to the Crimea . In fact she was still trooping at the time of the Boer war. In contrast to the *Dane* the *Himalaya* was huge, approximately eight times the tonnage of the smaller ship.

The R.M.S. Dane. 1855 - 1865. 530 gross tons. En route for the Cape.

The Dane was not only the Union Lines first mail ship; she was also the first to go on a pleasure cruise. The Captain and the Agents at Cape Town arranged this only a few days after the *Dane's* arrival on that first voyage. Some forty to fifty merchants of the city were invited to take a trip in the steamer to Hout Bay on the twelfth of November 1857. The trip was intended firstly to test whether some different coals were suitable and secondly to give the leading merchants an opportunity of seeing for themselves the sea going qualities of the ship. This trip was undoubtedly to advertise the new Company to all, and assure people that a new reliable mail, cargo and passenger service was in place, and that the Union Company would not fail after a few voyages, as had happened with other previous ventures.

The invited guests boarded the ship in the Bay to be welcomed by Captain Strutt and the agent. After a few words of welcome from the Captain, a first rate tiffin was provided. Shortly afterwards, the vessel weighed anchor and headed out of Table Bay. She followed the coastline and all admired the views of Table Mountain, the Lions Head and Signal Hill. Green Point and then Sea Point were passed, where many of the passengers were able to identify their own homes. The vessel was soon close in to Camps Bay and the grandeur of the Twelve Apostles was much admired. When the steamer reached Hout Bay, she was piloted by the Deputy Port Captain, and after steaming around the Bay so all on board could appreciate the view of the Sentinel and Chapmans Peak, the company sat down to dinner. After an excellent meal, which took some time, the ship again weighed anchor and started on the return journey. At 5.p.m. a very successful trip was concluded when the vessel arrived back in Table Bay and dropped anchor. The article that appeared in the 'Argus' following the excursion, described the *Dane* as a right good vessel. In addition the accommodation was described as not all that large but snug and comfortable.

Later the *Celt,* on her first visit to Cape Town, made a special trip as far as Port Elizabeth. This was to pick up Mqomo, a Xhosa Chief who was to be taken to the prison on Robben Island. True to say the Union Line quickly established itself on the Cape Run and for a number of years was able to withstand any opposition that appeared on the route. Improvements were soon made and it was only in the following year that passage rates for all classes included the use of bedding, mess utensils and a free rail pass from Southampton or Plymouth to London.

We tend to forget the difficulties that stood in the way of the Masters of these ships. There were few if any lighthouses anywhere on the coast in the early days. In addition the charts would not necessarily be all that reliable. Even in Table Bay in 1860 there were no lights on Robben Island or Moullie Point. There was a small tower at Green Point with two fixed lights, but that was all. We also tend to forget how tiny these early steamships were. The *Dane* for example was only 530 gross tons and was just 195 feet long.

For the passengers on these small ships the cabins were tiny. If one of the lady passengers was wearing a crinoline, there was literally no room to move in the cabin at all. In addition, the bunks were narrow, hard and uncomfortable. The best cabins were at the stern of the ship, where at least the passengers were some distance away from the heat of the furnaces in the engine room. The Second Class would have been very warm in what was called the fore cabin. When Third Class were carried, they would be nearer the bows of the ship. The compliment of passengers, taking the *Athens*, 739 tons of 1856 as an example, she would have carried seventy in the First Class with perhaps another thirty in Second Class and possibly another thirty in Third Class.

At that time there were no baths on board. However, when the decks were washed down in the early morning, a tub would be filled with seawater. Gentlemen only, could plunge into the tub between the hours of five and seven a.m. There is no mention of how the ladies managed, apart from the provision of a small bowl of water in the cabin. Later they were provided with a tub in the cabin, in which they could stand. The first Union ship provided with a bathroom for the First Class only joined the fleet in 1860. That year was an important one for the city of Cape Town, as the first tug from England named, the *Albatross* arrived in the harbour, and in addition, in the same year, the lighthouse at Cape Point was completed. This was not all, because Cape Town welcomed its first Royal visitor from England when Prince Alfred arrived on *H.M.S.Euryalus*. During his stay his most important engagement was to tip the first truck of stones for the new breakwater at Table Bay. As a result of this development, by 1870 the new Alfred Dock was completed in Cape Town and small though it was there was nothing to compare with it on either the western or eastern seaboard of Southern Africa. It was several months before the Union Line took advantage of the new dock as they continued to use the central pier. However, in November the *Saxon* became the Company's first ship to berth alongside the East quay.

Strangely enough in the early days, the victualling on the Union steamships was in the hands of the captain and not the Company. This lasted well into the 1870's. It is perhaps one of the reasons why, in all the advertisements in the Press, the name of the Master of the ship was included. Obviously the Captain's skills as Master and navigator were of prime importance. Some captains though, apparently provided a better table than others, and these ships were perhaps more popular than those where the fare was likely to be more frugal. Passengers today, used to a large and varied printed menu would look askance at the simple hand written cards that were produced on board up to around 1880.

As the Union Company prospered so the size of the ships increased. In 1860 the *Cambrian* became the first of the mail ships to exceed one thousand tons. Earlier in 1858, calls on the homeward voyage to St. Helena and Ascension had been added to the schedule. Despite pressure from Port Elizabeth to extend the mail service to Algoa Bay, it was some time before this occurred. However, when the two Rennies steamers, the *Waldensian* and the *Madagascar*, which provided a coastal service from Cape Town to Durban were both wrecked, the Union Line stepped in. This new enterprise by the Company was called the 'Intercolonial Service' and it began in February 1863. The *Norman*, having been replaced on the mail run, became the first Union ship to operate the new coastal service and was followed by the *Dane* and the *Anglian*. Later in the same year an addition to the calls at Port Elizabeth and Durban was made when a regular stop at the Buffalo River (East London) was added.

It was a year later in 1864 that a regular service between South Africa and Mauritius was started. Prior to this the trade had been carried mainly by a considerable number of small sailing vessels. They were able to offer lower

_The R.M.S. Cambrian 1860 - 1872. 1,055 gross tons. The first steamship
designed for the Cape run._

charges for freight and also could enter the smaller South African ports and go
alongside the quay or jetty. It was often the case that the larger steamers had to
anchor and discharge their cargo into lighters. A further year later, in October
1865 a mail contract was signed between the Natal government and the Union
Company. The coastal steamers with their shallow draught were used initially
to maintain this service.

In 1865, the Company also became involved, at least briefly, on the East
coast. The _Dane_, the first mail ship was chartered by the British Government
to be used to transport stores, supplies and reinforcements for the Naval ships
at Zanzibar. These warships were based at the island trying to arrest and seize
the slave dhows and others that were operating in that area. The presence of the
Navy in the waters around Zanzibar had been very effective. Sultan Majid of
Zanzibar, because of the British Navy's presence, planned a settlement on the
mainland at a tiny fishing village called Mzizma, meaning "Healthy Place",
which had an excellent natural harbour. The Sultan was a slave trader and as
his activities were being hindered by the British on the island of Zanzibar he
had decided to create a quiet base on the mainland. He decided to call the new
harbour Dar-es-Salaam meaning Haven of Peace. He sent thousands of slaves
there to build the palace and other buildings. Later, after slavery had been
abolished, the palace became a German prison.

Regrettably the *Dane* never reached Zanzibar as she was wrecked on Thunderbolt Reef near Port Elizabeth on her way from Simonstown. All on board were rescued but the ship became a total loss. It was to be some years later before the first Union ship reached Zanzibar.

A report in the Eastern Province Herald in December 1865 covered the official enquiry into the loss of the *Dane*. Captain Waldeck handed the following statement to the Resident Magistrate at Port Elizabeth. : - *'I was bound from Simons Bay with Government stores for Zanzibar and merely called in to land a Passenger and take the mails. From the hour we left Simons Bay up to the time of the unfortunate accident I was occupied with the ship, night and day, being anxious to use every precaution for the safety of all. I rounded Reciffe lighthouse, steering E.S.E., light bearing, N.N.E. distance five miles, with fresh winds from westward taking in sail all the while, and gave orders for two men at the wheel and one man in the chains. I attended to sailing directions given in De Hasey African Pilot, and made marginal notes as I came along the coast. I considered myself to be two and a half miles off the shore lighthouse bearing W.N.W., steering N.N.E. by N. I kept the lead constantly going and a short time before she struck the man gave us a cast of five fathoms and no bottom, which I examined. The next cast was three and a half fathoms, and she immediately struck. I kept a man in the chains till the state of the ship rendered it necessary to lower boats away, keeping three fathoms all the while. I considered I had judged the distance correctly. It is true I might have gone out further, but being clear weather and considering myself perfectly safe, and having to land only one passenger in Port Elizabeth and taking in the mails, I was anxious to proceed on my way the same evening. I therefore wished to go inside the Roman (Rock), if I had gone outside the Roman, I would not have been able to reach Algoa Bay the same evening, or at all events, not till very late that night, as it would have been a dead beat up. I may mention that the water appeared perfectly smooth within what I considered to be a mile and a half, certainly a mile and a quarter. In conclusion I can only say, since I have had command I have not for a moment neglected my duties, and have been most anxious for the safety of the ship and those entrusted to my care, and can safely appeal, in proof of this to any passengers or others who have sailed with me. I would also mention that there was no indication of danger, or any appearance on the water to let me think we were near a shoal.'*

Other evidence given in the course of the Enquiry showed that the ship was drawing fifteen feet aft and fourteen feet forward when leaving Simons Bay. It was also stated that as the *Dane* would have consumed a good deal of coal, estimated at sixteen tons, on the voyage she would have drawn less water.

The Magistrate said that in his opinion the Captain had made a great error of judgement in keeping too close inshore after rounding Cape Reciffe and that the loss of the ship was attributable to his default in not complying with the sailing directions for Algoa Bay. As no complaint was made against officers and crew, Mr. Skead Master R.N. as nautical assessor concurred with the Magistrates report. The judgement delivered was that the Captain's certificate be suspended for a period of twelve months.

At this time the Royal Navy's main base in the South Atlantic was at Simonstown and ships were operating from there up both the west and east coast of Africa in an endeavour to halt the slave trade. Many of the slave ships that were captured were brought to Simonstown and the Vice-Admiralty Courts sat regularly at the Cape to look into the cases against the dhows and other vessels that were brought in concerned with the carrying of slaves. One such Court in 1859 is recorded in the pages of the 'Argus'. It was concerned with ten dhows that had been captured by H.M.S. *Lyra*. They included the Muscat (Oman) dhow *Zabora* of 146 tons, a dhow taken off Comura (the Comores) of 112 tons, and four dhows taken in the Angoza river (Mozambique), two measuring 156 tons each, one of 168 tons and another 120 tons. In this instance the Attorney General appeared on behalf of the Portuguese Consul to take issue on the matter of the seizure of the dhows in the Angoza River. When they had been taken by the Navy, there had in fact been no slaves on board. However it was apparent that these dhows were being used in the slave trade. One of them, for example, had on board three hundred full water barrels. It appeared to be obvious, with this large quantity of water on board that she was indeed a slaver. This argument apparently won the day as some time later this dhow was advertised for sale in the newspaper complete with 300 water barrels. Many of the dhows, presumably those that could not find a buyer, were broken up on the beach at Simonstown. One, a captured Portuguese vessel *Eolo*, was sunk next to the Admiralty pier in Simonstown to strengthen it.

In December 1861 new harbour works were completed at Port Alfred, which had previously been called Port Frances. This was convenient for a number of towns in the area, the most important of which was Grahamstown. It was some time before the mail ships came any further than Cape Town. It was not until 1864 that they began to terminate at Port Elizabeth with the *Roman* taking the first mail sailing. The Union Line at that point decided to open their own Passenger and Freight office in the Port.

The coastal service provided a vital link for passengers, mail and freight bound for the ports up the coast. At this time there was no real alternative as travel overland was very slow and this did not change until the railways were built. The handling of both passengers and freight was difficult in these early days. Cape Town may have had its Alfred Dock but it was many long years before the other ports had similar facilities. Handling cargo in the roadstead at Algoa Bay (Port Elizabeth) was not easy if there was any sort of a sea running. Surf boats were used for both passengers and cargo, which were landed on the open beach. Algoa Bay was only a safe anchorage when the wind blew from the West. When a black South-Easter blew up all work ceased. Steamers were safe enough but sailing ships had to rely on their anchors to stop them drifting and ending up on the beach. When on occasion wind speeds reached up to eighty knots, then ships were lost and many of the crewmembers on board at the time were drowned. The situation only improved in 1881 when the North jetty was built. It was not until 1933 that Port Elizabeth had a harbour, which could handle all the Union-Castle ships.

Landing at East London could be even more difficult because of the swell. Passengers had to take their chance transferring to the tender using the ship's companion ladder. This was all very well for the pilots or agents who were well accustomed to this method of disembarking. For the women and children passengers and probably most of the men, this was a terrifying experience. This led eventually to a large basket being used. This was lowered by the ships derricks to transfer disembarking and boarding passengers from the tender. This was certainly a great improvement. For the ships themselves the mouth of the Buffalo River was also a poor anchorage when the southeast gales blew and over the years many ships were either badly damaged or wrecked. In the gale of the 26th May 1872 eight ships were driven ashore. As a result of that gale construction work began on a new harbour.

The bar at Durban was another major problem, which was not solved for many years, and a similar basket was used here for passengers. In 1864 the *Anglian* had been introduced on the coastal run. She was small, only 661 gross tons but she had a shallow draught and was able to enter both the Buffalo River and cross the bar at Durban. It was not until 1892 that the much larger intermediate ships were used, as it was then possible for them to berth alongside at the Point in Durban. The first of these was the *Dunrobin Castle* whose gross tonnage was 2,811.

It soon became the practice for the Union Line when trade was booming to slot in additional sailings to the Cape from Southampton. To differentiate between these vessels and the mail ships, they were described as extra or intermediate steamers. In time the term intermediate became used for any of the liners not employed on the mail service. In the early days ships were not built specifically as intermediates, they were mainly mail ships, which were either too slow or too old to remain on the mail run.

The long ocean voyage to the Cape created a number of problems. Bearing in mind that in the beginning the voyage was due to be completed in 42 days, as far as the mail contract was concerned, but of course if the weather was bad then the voyage could be longer. As time went on the voyage did become shorter as the ships were built with more powerful engines. However, the ports of call were limited to Madeira or the Canary Islands with possibly calls at Ascension and St. Helena. The amount of stores that could be obtained from most of these ports was limited. Certainly meat was difficult and most of the

The R.M.S. Dunrobin Castle. 1875-1893. 2,820 gross tons. Sailed for the Cape Verde Islands to cable news of the defeat of the British Army by the Zulu's

fresh meat that appeared on the menu was carried live. Refrigeration and cold storage were not to be available for some years to come. On board there would be sheep and chickens in various 'pens' so they might provide eggs and also for meat. On occasion some passengers would book a cabin in the Third Class for their own chickens to ensure they got their fresh eggs for breakfast. Tinned meat may have been carried as it had been available from the early years of the nineteenth century and possibly supplies would have been stocked on the ships if only for the First Class. For many years, presumably because of the Indian connection, curries appeared almost daily on the menu in addition to the usual roast joints.

There was a problem providing for children on board although milking cows were carried. These were normally kept on the fore deck with the chickens etc, taking up a lot of the space allocated to the Third Class passengers. Meals at the time were taken in the small saloon. Breakfast was at 9.a.m., lunch at noon, afternoon tea at 3.p.m. and dinner at 5 o'clock. Passengers had to squeeze onto hard benches in the saloon and once in your seat it was difficult to get out again no matter what crisis might arise. After dinner the passengers would spend the rest of the evening in the saloon playing cards or perhaps engaging in charades.

There was no lounge or smoking room in those days. In fact only on certain parts of the deck was smoking allowed. After dark this was only with the express permission of the captain. In the accommodation, smoking was not permitted at all, as everyone was very afraid of fire. The Union Line was quick to introduce improvements in the service. In 1858, stewardesses were appearing on the ships and in 1863 the first doctor was carried.

Bad weather can make shipboard life very uncomfortable at any time, even in the large liners of today fitted with stabilisers. On these small ships it could be a nightmare. An early account talks about dinner in the saloon in very rough weather. The joint of roast beef and gravy slid off the table into someone's lap on one side, being closely followed by the lamb and mint sauce on the other. Fiddle racks were used on the tables, to hold the crockery in place. Even: *"after three weeks on board the ship we were nearer South America than Africa and still being driven westward."* The report continues: *"I have never been in such a wretch of a ship, what with accidents, the rising of my bunk to fearful angles during the night, the crying of children and the breaking of glass makes life most uncomfortable. Our meals now are less plentiful and all the passengers are very hungry by dinner time."* The long sea voyage of thirty days or more in those early times could be a problem if bad weather caused a significant delay, which must have been the case in this instance. The captain was obviously conserving his dwindling food supplies. One would have thought he had enough to worry about with the bad weather and probably declining coal stocks as well. It is not surprising that the ships when they called at Madeira outward, and Cape Town homeward bound, topped up their coalbunkers for the long ocean voyage. They even had bags of coal stacked on deck to try to ensure that, whatever happened, they never ran out of fuel.

One of the major problems with the mail service in the early days was the time interval between the monthly sailings. It did not become twice monthly until the new mail contract came into force in 1870. As the homeward bound mail ship left Table Bay, only two days after the arrival of the inbound ship, only those living in Cape Town had an opportunity to reply to correspondence by return. As early as 1859 the Union Company was asked if they would introduce a new service from Cape Town, picking up mail for the United Kingdom at Port Elizabeth, East London and Durban and then sailing to Mauritius to connect with a monthly P & O. mail vessel from Australia bound for the Isthmus of Suez. The U.K. mail would be off loaded here and carried by rail overland from Suez to Alexandria then loaded on another P. & O. ship bound for Marseilles. Then again the mail that had paid the additional 4d surcharge above the normal rate of 1/- per ounce was once more carried by rail, then by cross - Channel packet to England. The remaining mail remained on board the ship and would arrive in England several days later. It was proposed that the Cape Colony should subsidise this venture but nothing came of it at that time.

Five years later, in 1864, the 'Overland Mail' service, as it was called, came into being. The Union Line mail ships took approximately 35 days from Cape Town to Southampton. The new Eastern route would take 46 days but it would still arrive in England well before the next Union mail ship. At this time Port Louis in Mauritius was an important 'cross roads' for shipping in the Indian Ocean as new routes were being opened to Australia, New Zealand and the Far East. This new overland service was well publicised by the Union Company in an attempt to encourage passengers to use this alternative route to and from Europe. The fares were made very competitive, as on the mail run at the time a First Class passage from Cape Town to Southampton was £111. On the new Eastern route the First Class fare to Mauritius was £25 and from there to England was £83.50. The overland section from Suez to Alexandria was an additional £2.50 also making a total of exactly £111. Bearing in mind that the voyage was eleven days or so longer on the new route, it was by comparison a bargain.

The *Athens* was the Union ship that began the new service in November 1864. When she arrived for the first time at Port Louis, some 150 of the local business community were invited on board for what was described as an 'excellent tiffin.' The *Anglian* and the *Cambrian* were also transferred on to this route. The *Athens* though was lost later in the great gale in Table Bay in May 1865 when sixteen ships were wrecked and others damaged. Many of the ships ran aground including the brigs *Galate* and *Jane* and the barques *Star of the West* and *Frederick Basil*. Two schooners also ended up on the beach and they were the *Clipper* and the *Ferndale*. The Union liner *Dane* was damaged when the barques *Alacrity* and *Deane* drifted, dragging their anchors and colliding with her. The *City of Peterborough* also dragged her anchor and went aground near Fort Knokke, close to the castle. The rocket brigade shot a line to her. The first attempt was wide but the second landed on the ship. After an interval the line was hauled back but there was no one attached. It was too late; all on board had already drowned.

The *Athens* had also broken loose from her moorings and she tried to ride out the storm at sea. As she rounded Mouille Point the seas were so bad that water cascaded into the engine room and doused the fires. Without her engines the ship was at the mercy of the elements. It was dark when the *Athens* struck midway between Green Point and Mouille Point lighthouses. By this time a crowd had gathered on the shore with ropes and lifebuoys but they were unable to help although loud cries could be heard from aboard the vessel. The ship was not much more than sixty yards from the shore and it was soon obvious that she was rapidly breaking up as debris was floating on to the beach.

The seas were tremendous and it seemed impossible that anyone could survive and reach the shore. This indeed was the case and all twenty-nine on board including the captain perished.

One of the cylinder heads from the engine of the *Athens* can still be seen from the shore. To see it so close makes one realise how violent the storm must have been if no one could be saved.

Within a matter of days the Cape newspapers were full of advertisements for all manner of goods that had been salvaged from the various ships and were for sale. All sorts of items were included from hogsheads of wine to bales of wool and hides. In addition many of the ships that had run aground were also up for sale.

The new route to Mauritius was not altogether successful. The main problem at certain times of the year was the weather on the South African coast, which could delay the ships on their way to the island. This meant that sometimes they missed the connection at Port Louis and the mail and any passengers had to wait there for another month. In addition, it was soon decided that Mauritius was no longer the right place for such a hub for different routes. So P. & O. stopped calling at Port Louis and went to Galle instead, the main port of Ceylon at the time. For two years the Union Company continued with this new arrangement, still calling at Mauritius on the way to Galle. By then the ships operating on this route were the *Mauritius, Natal* and *Dane*.

In 1868 the existing mail contract was extended for a further six years from 1870 to 1876. The only change being that the service became twice monthly. This meant there was now no need for the additional mail service to England via Galle. Added to which, the Mauritius government did not want to continue to pay its share of the subsidy. The service, therefore, to Mauritius and Galle was terminated that year. This meant that the Line now had surplus ships and the *Mauritius* and *Dane* were sold with only the *Natal* being retained. The Union Line did not renew regular sailings to the island until 1891 when the *Arab* took the first sailing.

In the beginning, the service to Mauritius had been profitable because sugar cane was grown extensively on the island. The sugar was by far the most important cargo brought back to South Africa. When the cane fields in Natal began to be developed, sugar from Mauritius and the route became unprofitable with very little cargo carried on the return voyage from the island.

In November 1869 the Empress Eugenie opened the Suez Canal and the first convoy of sixty-seven ship made the voyage from Port Said to Suez to celebrate the event. At the time it was thought that this would mean a decline in the number of ships sailing via the Cape as the steamers and other vessels from India and the Far East would take the shorter route to the United Kingdom and Europe. However, the sailing ships found that the cost of using the canal was too high as they had to be towed through by tugs. The vast majority therefore still sailed via Cape Town to India, Australia and the Far East. Even some of the steamship companies initially seemed reluctant to change but this did not last for long. A further factor was the discovery of diamonds at

Kimberley in the Northern Cape, which brought a rush of prospectors seeking their fortunes. There were around 10,000 prospectors at the diggings but the new discovery brought in another 50,000. This approximately doubled the population of both the Transvaal and the Orange Free State. With space for both passengers and cargo at a premium this in its turn brought about an increase in the number of ships, at least for the time being, calling at the Cape. The effect of the opening of the canal was only to be felt at a later date.

In 1871 the Union Line coaster *Natal* towed into Port Elizabeth a schooner, the *Thomas Nickerson* which had been anchored off the mouth of the Gouritz River near Mossel Bay. There was no one on board but there were signs that there might have been a mutiny. Guns and cutlasses littered the deck and the captain's cabin had obviously been ransacked and all the ships papers were missing. She was a Russian ship and was bound for Yokohama in Japan with a full cargo. Some days later the first mate of the vessel and some seaman arrived in Port Elizabeth. Their story was that the ship had started to leak badly in gale force winds. They had found shelter in the river mouth and having dropped anchor, they then abandoned her. They went on to say that two boats were launched and the one carrying the Captain and the other members of the crew drowned when their boat overturned in the heavy seas. The officials at Port Elizabeth were not convinced by the story. Why were all the arms scattered on the deck? However, no further survivors were found and nothing could be proved.

In 1873 the Union Company introduced a new coaster the *Namaqua* to operate on the West coast. She was small, only 352 gross tons but she was destined for the Cape Town to Port Nolloth service. She carried the copper ore from Namaqualand back to Cape Town for transshipping. The service only lasted three years as she ran aground South of Handeklip Bay and was wrecked.

Serious competition for the Union Line did not really surface until Donald Currie appeared on the scene. He was born in Greenock in Scotland in 1825. He was educated in Belfast but returned to Greenock in 1839 where he was employed in a shipping office. Three years later he joined his brother James Currie in the Liverpool office of the Cunard Line, which was then the only Company providing a regular service of steamers between England and North America. On the final abolition of the Navigation Laws in 1849, Currie was sent by the Cunard Line to open branch offices for them on the continent. After returning to Liverpool he became head of the Cunard Line's freight department until 1862. It was then that he started business on his own account, and founded the Donald Currie Line.

Although Currie had many connections in the United States he would not enter into competition with his former employees, but started a sailing ship service to Calcutta. Originally he operated from the Mersey. After he left Cunard he transferred to the Thames with his Head Office at 52, Lime Street.

In 1869 he established the Liverpool and Hamburg Steam Ship Company, managed by Donald Currie & Company. Two years later he had started to build steam ships for the India route. It was then that Donald Currie chartered two of his ships to George Payne who was trying to compete with the Union Line on the Cape Route. The two ships were the *Iceland* and the *Gothland,* but within weeks Payne told Currie that he would not be able to meet the cost of the charter. This meant that Donald Currie was forced to take over the risk of the voyages himself and, with encouragement from merchants in South Africa, almost by accident, Currie came into long term competition with the Union Line. Soon afterwards he moved to larger premises in Fenchurch Street in the City, which remained the Head Office of first, the Castle Line and then Union-Castle until the latter half of the 1950's.

The Castle steamers to begin with only carried private mails as the Union Company had the mail contract. To gain an advantage, Currie's ships final port of call in the United Kingdom was Dartmouth to pick up passengers and the mail. The ships sailed three days before the Union mail ship left Southampton. As Currie's ships were designed for speed they usually reached Cape Town up to ten days ahead of their rivals. Apart from the Castle ships being faster the cost per letter was less than half the price charged by the mail ship. The *Lapland* was used on this service initially in 1873 and later she was employed on the South African coast. Six years later the ships were sailing to Mauritius. One of Currie's vessels was the *Elizabeth Martin*. From 1872 she ran as a mail ship for three years and following this she was placed on the coastal service between Cape Town and Durban where she inaugurated a new service to Port Alfred.

Currie's new line was advertised in the United Kingdom as the 'Colonial Mail Line" and in South Africa as the 'London Line' to make it clear that this had no connection with the Union Company and that the ships were based in London not Southampton. In South Africa they were also referred to as the 'Dartmouth Boats' as this was the final port of departure from England where the mails were taken on board. Currie gained a further advantage in the early days by arranging for his ships to call at Bordeaux outward bound, which at this time was as far South as the new telegraph reached. His ships were able to pick up the latest news from London and to get it to Cape Town well in advance of the Union line mail ships.

As early as 1870 a proposal had been made in the Cape that there should be a Round Africa service operated by the Union Company. It was thought that this could help in persuading the Sultan of Zanzibar to ban the trade in slaves. As a result of this the United Kingdom postal authorities were instructed to see if it would be possible to establish regular steamship sailings, one from the Cape or Durban to Zanzibar and the other from Aden. The Union Company were approached but were not too happy to operate such a service without a subsidy. They did point out to the government that ships of a shallow draught would be needed and it was impossible to forecast how much trade there would be as the East coast was largely unknown. They wrote proposing a monthly service between Cape Town and Zanzibar for which they would need an annual subsidy of £29,000

Later, another offer was received from the British India Company stating that they would provide both services, Aden to Zanzibar and on to Cape Town for a subsidy of £27,365. When the Union Line found out about this quote, they started negotiations with British India. This culminated in the two companies sending in a joint quotation splitting the service and the Union Line had reduced its quote to £15,000.

All this was going on at a time when the Union Line became aware that Donald Currie was poised to enter into competition on the Cape run. The British government never had the Zanzibar agreement ratified by the Cape Legislative Assembly. The Union Company did not realise that this could be a problem and went ahead ordering new ships for the Zanzibar route, together with new mail boats and other older ships were to be re-engined This was because part of the deal that had been struck meant that the existing mail contract would be extended for a further three and a half years taking it to 1881. This would effectively block Currie. By the end of 1872 the facts were leaked and there was an immediate outcry in both the Cape and in London, stirred up by Donald Currie. The Zanzibar contract was eventually confirmed but the extension of the Southampton to Cape Town mail contract was not. When it came up again in 1876, Currie also tendered for the contract and it was decided the Union and Castle Lines should share the mail service jointly.

Since the opening of the Alfred Dock in Cape Town very little had happened elsewhere. In December 1861 new harbour works were completed in Port Alfred and for a time from 1875 both Union and Castle Line ships called regularly at the port. The Union ship was the *Basuto* and the Castle line vessel was the *Elizabeth Martin*. Later on in the 1880's even the mail ships called but not on a regular basis. However, by 1889 both companies stopped calling because of the better port facilities at Port Elizabeth. Port Alfred then went into permanent decline and in 1915 the port was officially closed.

Some improvements had been made over the years. In 1878 the Union Line sailed out the *Union*, the first tug to be used at Durban. For this voyage only she was rigged as a topsail schooner and the journey took her 45 days. When she arrived the masts and sails were removed, as they were no longer required. She was eventually lost in 1894 when she went aground on the bar at Chinde in Portuguese East Africa.

In 1873 a direct intermediate service to Port Elizabeth had started and the *Syria* took the first sailing. It was not though a very auspicious voyage as the ship broke her prop shaft in the South Atlantic and proceeded initially under

19

sail before being towed to the U.K.

In the same year the Zanzibar service was started with the *Natal*. Beforehand she was overhauled in Cape Town and was painted principally yellow and white instead of the normal black. It may have been that the directors thought this was a more appropriate colour because of the heat and humidity on the East Coast. The success of this was possibly the reason that at a later date the Union Company changed the colour of their mail ships to yellow and white

Prior to the *Natal's* first sailing, she did a short cruise to Saldanha Bay with a number of local dignitaries on board. Shortly afterwards on her return to Cape Town she set off on her first voyage to Zanzibar. When she reached the island she found that *H.M.S. Enchantress* was anchored off Stone Town whilst the emissary from the British Government was trying to persuade the Sultan to abolish the slave trade. Although the attempt failed , later the same year Sultan Seyid Barghash did prohibit the slave trade within his dominions. The slave market at Zanzibar was closed and in the 1880's the Anglican cathedral was built on the site.

The *Natal* was joined on this new service by the *Basuto* and the *Kafir* and later the *Zulu*. The *Kafir* had been the first Union ship to call at *Delgoa* Bay. Later the *Basuto* and the *Zulu* were sold, and in 1878 the *Kafir* was wrecked in False Bay, some nine miles from Cape Point. Some of those on board managed to get ashore and raise the alarm and a rider was sent to Simonstown. By this time sea conditions had worsened and it became impossible to launch the boats and later the ship broke in half. Next morning when help arrived all on board were rescued with the exception of four members of the crew including the Chief Officer. As a mark of esteem, and in recognition of his former gallantry in saving life, the Company's officers erected a memorial to the memory of the Chief Officer, Charles Merritt. The memorial can be found in St. George's Cathedral in Cape Town.

One of the early problems for those visiting Zanzibar was the drinking water. Over the years there had been numerous outbreaks of cholera, which had killed thousands of people. Sultan Bargash put an end to this by bringing a pipeline from Bububu (the place of the bubbling water) to the town so that everyone could drink pure clean water. It was the cleanest water anywhere on the coast and it was especially famous among shipping people in those early days because it was pure and free. Even up to the 1950's many ships would take on water at Zanzibar because of its high quality. Regretfully in more recent years the bubbling water has stopped flowing and now in times of drought the island has to bring in tanker loads of fresh water from the mainland.

The Zanzibar route became an intermediate service from Southampton in 1880 and four of the older mail ships were transferred to operate it. The ships were the *Danube, Roman, Teuton and Nyanza*. The last named had been launched as a paddle steamer in 1864 for the P. & O. Line and used on the Southampton to Alexandria run. This tied up with the overland route via Suez to the East. She became surplus to requirements once the Suez Canal opened and she was bought by the Union Line in 1873. She was converted to a single screw vessel and her two funnels were reduced to one. She was originally used on the mail run until she was placed on the Zanzibar service. Although the vessels normally only went as far as Zanzibar on some voyages they did also call at Mombasa.

The Union Line went through a bad patch after the deal fell through over the mail contract extension. The new ships had been ordered and the total bill was over £335,000, a very large sum at the time.

That year the Company failed to pay a dividend to its shareholders and once these ships were completed no more were built for five years.

An early account of a voyage on the *Edinburgh Castle* in 1878 refers to the embarkation at Algoa Bay where passengers with all their baggage were taken out to the vessel in large sailing lighters. After dark the only lighting inside the accommodation was provided by candles inserted into holders that swung with the motion of the ship.

When the *Edinburgh Castle* reached Cape Town she docked in the Alfred Basin, which at that time was the only completed part of the docks. The breakwater for the new Victoria Basin had already been started although it had not reached any great length. On the opposite wharf was the *German* and in the berth next door to the *Edinburgh Castle* was the *Florence*. The *Melrose* was also in port.

The next port of call was St. Helena where the vessel arrived after dark. Firing off a brass canon and a display of rockets signalled their approach. After leaving the island, the next land passed was Cape Verde, which could be seen clearly. Later, further north, the ship passed a small brig wallowing in the seas that was flying the Yellow Fever flag. A stop was made at Madeira where the boys diving for silver coins entertained the passengers. After twenty-one days the *Edinburgh Castle* anchored in Plymouth Sound where the passengers disembarked.

In 1878 the *Taymouth Castle*, an extra steamer, joined the fleet. For twelve months she filled in on the mail run because of the loss of the *Windsor Castle*. In 1878 the *Duart Castle* also became an extra steamer.

It was at the very beginning of the year 1879 that Britain found itself at war with the Zulu nation. Within three weeks of the war starting, on the 22nd of January, the British Army suffered one of its worst defeats when they were routed by the Zulu Impis at Isandlwana. The British forces were overwhelmed by thousands of King Cetawayo's warriors. This left the city of Durban virtually undefended and the citizens were extremely worried. This was because of the threat that King Cetawayo had made that he would come to the

Port and put out the big candle that shone from the harbour bluff.

The first news of the disastrous defeat soon reached Cape Town. The *African,* a Union Line mail ship was in port and Captain Crutchley, her Commander, quickly realised that reinforcements would be needed as soon as possible. There were troops in Cape Town and he offered his ship, with the agreement of the agent, to the Government to convey the soldiers to Durban. This was quickly agreed and the ship was hastily prepared to embark the troops. As soon as they were on board, the *African* sailed for Natal. She made a good passage, calling at Algoa Bay without anchoring. She did however stop briefly at East London before reaching Durban. The troops were put ashore, together with one of the *African's* signal guns to join the defensive line around the port. Shortly afterwards the Union Line steamer *Nyanza* arrived at Durban where she embarked 150 women and children that had been evacuated from Pietermaritzburg. They were taken back to safety in Cape Town

By this time the Castle liners, *Courland* and *Dunkeld* had arrived in Cape Town and were made available to carry more troops with their guns and equipment to Port Natal. The homeward bound mail ship, the *Dunrobin Castle,* sailed early for England to carry the news of the disaster. She steamed flat out to reach St. Vincent in the Cape Verde Islands. By then the telegraph had reached this far south from London and they were able to cable the bad news ahead. The facts about the massacre at Isandlwana reached London at least a week earlier than would otherwise have been the case.

Donald Currie was quick to act when he got the news. The next mail ship due to sail from Southampton was a Union Line ship. Currie passed all the information on to the British government and cabled the *Conway Castle,* which had already left England, at Madeira. He instructed the Captain to call at St. Vincent on her way south to pick up the latest news about reinforcements and their probable date of arrival at Durban. This meant that the news of the Governments intentions reached Durban much sooner.

On the same day, the 11th February, that the news reached England, the Union Line mail ship, *Pretoria* steamed into Southampton from the Cape. All on board were completely unaware of what had happened in Natal. She was quickly converted into a troopship so that she could be used to carry nearly a thousand men of the 91st Highlanders regiment to Durban. In addition there were other passengers on board bringing the total on board the ship to 1,200. The *Pretoria* sailed from Southampton only eight days after her arrival on the 19th February. There were thousands on the quayside to see her off. Before the ship left, provision had already been made for disembarking at Durban, a somewhat risky affair. The troops would be stowed in large barges outside the bar, and then dragged through the surf before landing.

Lady Barker, in her *'Years Housekeeping in South Africa'* book gives a vivid description of crossing the bar in those early days. *'The next five minutes hold a peril in every second. 'Scrape, scrape, scrape! We've struck. No we haven't! Helm hard down. Over! And so we are. Among the breakers it is true, knocked to one side and then the other, buffeted here, and buffeted there, but we keep right on, and a few more turns of the screw take us into calm water under the hills of the Bluff.'*

The R.M.S. Pretoria 1878 - 1897. 3,199 gross tons. Leaving Southampton with troops bound for Natal, 19th February 1879.

The *Pretoria* steamed at full speed without calling at the other Cape ports and she arrived at Durban in 24 days and 8 hours, a record passage that stood for many years. She had arrived ten days earlier than would have been the case if Donald Currie had not taken such prompt action.

The *Dublin Castle* was also requisitioned and quickly converted. The interior of the ship had been transformed. All the ordinary fittings, save the cooking galleys had gone.

Rows of mess tables had been put down, and beams dotted with strong iron hooks for swinging the hammocks. A Hospital, Dispensary and Prison were also fitted up.

The Dublin Castle. 1877 - 1882. 2,805 gross tons. Departing Gravesend with troops bound for the Cape.

The troops due to sail on the *Dublin Castle* were 740 men of the 60th Rifles. While waiting for the ship to come from the South West India Docks, the troops stood at ease on Gravesend Pier. As in Southampton many relatives, friends, and others had turned up to see the ship sail. Those who could afford it paid a penny to go on the pier to mingle with the soldiers. Soon the *Dublin Castle* arrived, a splendid ship wearing a new coat of French grey paint. The ferry *Earl of Essex* took the troops to the ship anchored in the river. In less than two and a half hours all the men were aboard and she sailed for Natal on the 19th February.

Another transport sailed from Gravesend later in the week. She was the *Manora* of the British India Line. She embarked 241 officers and men of the 6th Brigade of the Royal Artillery and one hundred horses. The embarkation of the horses attracted much attention from the bystanders. The horses were blindfolded before being led into a cage, which was then lifted by crane and lowered on to the main deck. It took only just over one and a half hours to transfer the one hundred horses on to the ship. Other Union Line ships were also used to carry troops, including the *Asiatic, Teuton* and *American.*

A troopship outward bound. The officers take a bath with the help of the crew.

The Union liner *Danube* sailed for the Cape shortly afterwards and amongst her passengers was the Prince Imperial of France, the son of the Emperor Napoleon III and Empress Eugenie. The Prince was the heir to the throne but the Emperor had been deposed in 1870 when France had been declared a Republic. The Prince was on his way to Durban to join Lord Chelmsford who

24

The 60th Rifles arriving at The Point, Durban.

was the British Army Commander. Within a few weeks the Prince, on a patrol in Zululand, had been ambushed and killed. He had tried to vault onto his horse but the saddle slipped, throwing him to the ground, where he was speared to death by Zulu warriors.

Within three months the war was over. King Cetawayo had been defeated and captured by the British forces. With his wives and attendants he was taken to the small harbour of Port Dunford, which was north of Durban where the Union Line coaster *Natal* was waiting. The King, and his family were embarked and they were housed in a Kraal that had been specially built for them on the poop deck. The *Natal* sailed for Simonstown and when she arrived the King was transferred to the Castle at Cape Town. He stayed in exile in the Cape until 1882 when he went to London. The following year he returned to Zululand where he died in February 1884.

Less than a year after the war ended normal services to South Africa were resumed. The *Dartmouth and Brixham Chronicle* at the time carried much interesting information about the Castle Line, as the ships called at Dartmouth outward bound to take on the mails.

The newspaper refers to the favourite steamship of the Line. - *"The Dublin Castle, J.D. Jefferies, R.N.R. Commander, arrived from London this morning at 5 o'clock, having been detained in the docks for 24 hours, in consequence of the Bank holiday. She has a large and valuable general cargo, for Cape Town, Mossel Bay, Algoa Bay, the Kowie, East London, Natal and Mauritius.*

The Dublin Castle takes goods for the Mauritius, to be transhipped to the Elizabeth Martin at Cape Town. The Edinburgh Castle will take goods for Algoa Bay direct, East London and Natal. The Dunrobin Castle will take passengers and mails for Mauritius, for conveyance by Branch mail steamer. The Kinfauns Castle will take goods for Mauritius to be transhipped to the Lapland at the Cape.

Letters for these ships must be addressed 'via Dartmouth', and can be posted at the Dartmouth office up to Friday, before 11 a.m. postage 6d per half ounce. Letters for the steamships leaving on Saturdays may be posted at Dartmouth up to 11 a.m. on Saturdays.

The steamship Kinfauns Castle which left Cape Town on Wednesday the 10th (a heavy South East gale having prevented her from leaving on the 9th) and Madeira on the 28th, passed up Channel, for London, on Tuesday afternoon, after a passage of 20 days 4 hours from Cape Town to Plymouth Sound. She brought 111 passengers, 36 bags and one packet of mails and a full general cargo.

The Taymouth Castle, R. Rigby, Commander (an extra steamer) which left Cape Town on the 2nd, and Madeira on the 20th, passed up Channel for London on Friday morning after a passage of 23 days 8 hours. She brought a full general cargo, 10 passengers, and 3 sacks of mails."

The Castle Line ships ceased to call at Dartmouth in 1891. Calling at Plymouth to take on the mails for East Africa was resumed later, when the intermediates were sailing through the Mediterranean to Mombasa, Dar-es-Salaam etc. A postcard from the *Gaika*, dated 1913 shows that a passenger on the ship went from Plymouth to East Africa on her. She called at Gibraltar, Marseilles. Port Said and Aden en route.

On the 1st January 1880, direct cable communication to the Cape from Britain was eventually established via Aden.

CHAPTER 2 - RIVALRY BETWEEN UNION AND CASTLE

It was in December 1880 that the first Boer war broke out between Britain and the Transvaal. The English population in the towns were beleaguered and the Boers drove off a relieving force from Natal. Later a British Force made a night ascent of Majuba Hill. At dawn the next day they were attacked by the Boers and because the British ran out of ammunition, most were either killed or wounded. This effectively ended the war and peace was made and the Republic of Transvaal was recognised by the British government. Again troops were sent out from Britain on the *Pretoria*. She sailed direct to Durban arriving in nineteen days, a new record.

In the same year the Union Line once again had a Royal passenger when the Empress Eugenie, whose son the Prince Imperial of France had been killed in Zululand, chose to travel with the Union Line on their new ship, the *German*. She sailed out on her to Durban and because of the difficulties in landing at the port a special basket was made to lower the Empress and her entourage into the tender. This was then used by all passengers landing or embarking at Durban. It was so successful that quite soon similar baskets were in general use at East London, Port Elizabeth and later Mossel Bay. The Empress visited the site in Zululand where the Prince had died.

She returned to England on the *Trojan*, which was on its maiden voyage. When the liner reached St. Helena, the Empress was able to visit Longwood, the house where Napoleon had lived during his exile, and she also visited the site of his tomb that was not far away.

To take passage on these ships in the early years was a true adventure. Quite early on they were being described as floating hotels but by our standards today even the First Class would appear rather 'Spartan'. Dependent on the state of the tide, embarkation could be comparatively easy when the ship was berthed alongside in the inner dock in Southampton or alongside the quay at Blackwall in the East India Dock. If it was a case of going out to the ship on a small tug or tender at Southampton, it could be quite unpleasant in bad weather. Once the passengers were on board, together with their steamer trunks, portmanteaux and hatboxes, the ship was soon under way.

In some respects nothing seems to have changed. A contemporary account on a Castle steamship describes the first dinner on board and how many of the passengers did not appear, as they were indisposed. It even describes how the more fortunate could hear the ominous sounds of human beings in distress as the meal progressed. This is not altogether surprising as at that time the First Class cabins were on either side of the saloon and opened directly on to it.

Status on board as a passenger, was governed by your seat in the dining saloon. The most important and influential would be seated either side of the captain. If you were placed at the lower end of the table ('below the salt' as it might have been called in the distant past) then you were considered of little account. The younger gentlemen would not be too disappointed and would perhaps resort to a small bribe to try to gain a place next to one of the unattached young ladies. As it was charmingly put at the time, *"Nautical morality is not straight laced, all tight lacing is injurious especially on board an ocean going steamer."* Again, nothing much seems to have changed over the past one hundred and twenty five years or more. As the voyage was so long it could become very boring for the passengers. There was little to do to while away the time although, having said that, the Victorians were well accustomed to providing their own entertainment. Concerts were particularly popular with many of the passengers doing their "party piece". Even the Captain might take part. One such on the Castle Line was an extremely good flautist. The ports of call were few and therefore provided a welcome diversion. The first stop was often at the island of Madeira. The Captain, whenever he appeared, would be questioned closely as to when the ship would arrive. Exactly the same thing tends to happen on board ship today. Why is it that once having taken passage in a ship, we want to know as soon as possible when we can get off it again?

Funchal is the capital of the island of Madeira and if the ship arrived late in the day, the coaling would be delayed until the following morning. This would mean there would be an opportunity for the passengers to go ashore in daylight to explore this Portuguese colony. In any event, no one wanted to be on board while coaling was going on, as the dust and dirt tended to get everywhere. This is one reason why many passengers at the time still preferred to travel on sailing ships. They could not stand the dust and grime that is inevitable on board a coal-burning steamer. This was at its worst when in port taking on coal.

In Madeira the coaling usually took about five or six hours, plenty of time to have a good look round the town. Carriages drawn by bullocks and the famous sledges were available for hire and there would be a chance to buy wickerwork, lace and perhaps a few bottles of Madeira wine. All too soon, the passengers would rejoin the liner, where they would be entertained before the ship sailed, by the local boys diving into the crystal clear waters of the bay for silver coins, until eventually the ship would haul up her anchor and be on her way again heading south into warmer waters.

By 1880 the Castle Line was well established on the South African coast with three vessels. These were the *Melrose*, *Venice* and *Dunkeld*. Although the mail service up the coast was now weekly, there was still a need for these coasters for both passengers and cargo. Later on, these vessels occasionally went beyond Durban to Delgoa Bay (Lourenco Marques) and other smaller ports in Mozambique. The smaller coasters were also used for the minor ports. Mossel Bay was one where these ships called regularly until the new railway line to Cape Town was completed. Much later the mail ships used to call here as the need arose.

At first the arrival of the mail ship at Cape Town was signalled by two guns being fired from the ship as she anchored. Later, an earlier indication was given by the flying of a flag from Signal Hill. There was a code of signals for different Company ships and also for indicating where the ships were from. The sighting of the mail ship was signalled first when she hove in sight, and then on her arrival in Table Bay, by a blue and white chequered flag. When she anchored, the whole town would know by the gunfire that the mail was in. Later Company house flags were hoisted. The firing of a single gun signalled the departure of the mail ship.

This practice of signalling the arrival of ships from Signal Hill ceased just before the beginning of the First World War. In the 1880s the intermediate vessels took over the calls at St. Helena and Ascension from the mail ships. This lasted until 1967 when the last intermediate was withdrawn. In the early days the steamers did not always maintain their schedules. Often the arrival at St. Helena would be at night. In order to let the islanders know of the ships arrival both the guns on board would be fired and rockets launched.

Increasing trade with South Africa caused both Union and Castle Lines to provide occasional intermediate sailings, and by 1881 both companies were maintaining weekly services to the Cape. In 1883 both the *Conway Castle* and *Dunrobin Castle* were transferred to the intermediate service. The latter vessel was the first Castle liner to have the First Class dining saloon extending the full width of the ship.

However, with the beginning of the depression many of these steamers were laid up. It was 1889 before the situation improved and intermediate sailings re-appeared. It was thought at one time that an intermediate vessel was something between a mail ship and a cargo boat, but neither Line had cargo boats before 1898.

By 1880 the small ships that had pioneered the Zanzibar route, were replaced by larger steamers, the *Nyanza, Danube, Roman* and *Teuton*. All of these had been mail ships at one time. The *Nyanza* only completed one voyage as the Sultan of Zanzibar was so taken by the appearance of the ship that he purchased her from the Union Line for his own private yacht. The name was never changed and at times she was used to carry passengers and cargo to and from Bombay. Even when she was too old for service, the Sultan would not part with her. She lay at anchor off Stone Town for many years and was not finally scrapped until 1904.

By 1880 the ships on the Zanzibar run left Cape Town once a month and the sailings were well advertised beforehand in the Cape newspapers. One such sailing was by the *Anglian,* which was due to call at Delgoa Bay, Inhambane, Quelimane, Mozambique and finally Zanzibar. As the time approached for the steamer to sail the advertisement in the 'Argus' stated that: - " *The R.M.S. Anglian will leave for Zanzibar as soon as possible after the arrival of the Mail ship Arab from the United Kingdom."*

The *Teuton*, whilst on the Zanzibar run was sunk with heavy loss of life. She had left Cape Town on her way to Port Elizabeth when she struck a rock off Quoin Point because she had strayed off course. The captain decided to turn back as there appeared to be no immediate danger. The weather was fine and he set a course for Simonstown. She was holed and taking in water but the bulkheads were holding. The pumps were manned by the crew and some of the passengers, and in addition all was made ready to abandon ship if it became necessary. Three hours later, when night had fallen, the ship was slowing down as she was starting to sink by the head. The order was given to abandon ship. The first boat was safely launched but the bulkheads in the liner suddenly gave way and the ship went down. Within one minute she had disappeared altogether. The only people saved were the thirty-six in the first lifeboat. The remaining 236 on board were drowned.

At this time in the period before Christmas, the shops in Cape Town would advertise the arrival of special shipments for the festive season. One such advertisement a few days before Christmas included: Roast Pheasant, Roast Partridge, Roast Fowl, Cooked Hams and Bacon, Jugged Hare, Pilchards in oil, Imperial hot Pickle, Calves foot jelly and Persian sherbet. One hundred and Eight cases in all just arrived per Dublin Castle.

Although baskets had been introduced at Durban and elsewhere, even so disembarking at these ports could still be a harrowing experience. An account written in the 1880's describes the use of the basket at Durban.

'When the steam tender arrives alongside the ship to take off disembarking passengers, a large basket is used to lower people over the side into the tender. With the ship rolling heavily it was a terrible ordeal for anyone of a nervous disposition. The passengers entered the basket through a door, then, using the ship's winch, it was lifted from the deck and lowered over the side. It was then a case of waiting for the right moment to drop the basket onto the deck of the tender. This could take several minutes while the basket swung to and fro like a pendulum. When the moment came, the basket was dropped quickly onto the deck of the tender often arriving with considerable force. Having got on board the tender a further trial awaited the passengers. The bar had to be crossed which was nearly always an unpleasant experience. The passengers would be put into the small cabin while the tender rolled viciously as the bar was negotiated. One wonders how, when it was a matter of climbing down a rope ladder to disembark, that many passengers got ashore at all'.

It was a good many years before the basket was finally dispensed with. At Durban it was 1892 before the intermediates could cross the bar and berth alongside. Another twelve years were to pass before the first mail ship berthed in the port. In Port Elizabeth the *Llandaff Castle* was berthed in 1934, to be followed shortly afterwards by the first of the mail ships. East London had to wait even longer. The first intermediates entered the port in 1893 but the Castle Line 'D' ships were too big and did not enter until 1914. In 1927 the *Llanstephan Castle* became the largest of the Company's ships to berth in the harbour and it was a further ten years before all the mail ships followed suit

The Zanzibar contract terminated in 1881 and it was not renewed as it was considered by then that the slave trade had ended, and therefore the British Government would not provide a fresh subsidy. As far as the Union Line were concerned, without the subsidy the service would run at a loss so it was discontinued.

With the Zanzibar contract at an end, the Union Line had sufficient ships available to have fortnightly intermediate sailings from Southampton. This meant that with the Company's mail ships they had a regular weekly service to South Africa. The Malay Muslim community in the Cape made good use of this service up the coast while it lasted. They would travel via Zanzibar to Aden at the time of the annual pilgrimage to Mecca and return the same way. Previously it had been very difficult if not impossible to make this pilgrimage. This was something that happened for many, many years. When the service was renewed later, the pilgrims returned and were still travelling on the Union-Castle ships to Aden and back well into the 1950's.

In 1881 the Union Line sent one of their intermediate steamers to Hamburg once a month to take on cargo bound for South Africa. Later on, the ships also called at Antwerp. By 1887 calls at Rotterdam and Flushing were added, to pick up passengers. This was introduced to encourage Dutch settlers to come out to the Transvaal. This same year gold was discovered and the recession was over.

An account of a voyage on a Union Line steamer in the 1880's, describes how the headwaiter and the stewards decorated the saloon for Christmas Day. They had some mistletoe and other greenery together with rosettes of many different colours. Paper chains were also used to give the saloon a festive appearance. On New Years Eve the Captain provided some entertainment for the passengers with a magic lantern show. He also had what is described as a small hand organ. This seems to have been a type of pianola as it was played by feeding in lengths of paper pricked with the notes. Some of the sheets were torn which gave the melodies a 'somewhat intoxicated character'. The evening was further enlivened by several bowls of iced champagne punch. This seems to have created the right atmosphere for a general singsong to take place, culminating at midnight with all the company joining hands to sing Auld Lang Syne.

By 1881 the Castle Line had established itself to the point where it went public as the Castle Mail Packet Company Limited. Only a few days later Donald Currie was knighted by the Queen. This was largely because of his prompt actions during the Zulu war in 1879. A few days later on the 23rd July

1881 many distinguished guests joined Sir Donald on board the *Garth Castle* at the East India Docks in London. They were to sail on the ship, which had been named after Sir Donald Currie's estate in Scotland, to celebrate the opening of a new Dock at Leith, the port for Edinburgh. When they arrived off Leith they joined the Naval Squadron commanded by the Duke of Edinburgh and the vessels all steamed in to the anchorage. That evening, a banquet was held on the *Garth Castle*, the principal guests being the Duke of Edinburgh and Prince Henry of Prussia. It was the Duke, who at the conclusion of the dinner proposed a toast to their host, Sir Donald and also congratulated him on receiving his Knighthood.

Beginning in 1883 a severe recession hit South Africa. The Castle Line built no ships for seven years after the *Methven Castle* appeared, and in the same period, the Union Line only built four coasters. Both lines suspended their intermediate services for a time and many of the ships were laid up. The prime mover for establishing the South African Shipping Conference, was the Castle Company and a number of companies joined this, including the Union Line. It proved to be of considerable benefit while the recession lasted.

In 1883 Sir Donald Currie bought a steamer of around 4,000 tons while it was still being built at Barrow-in-Furness. She was named the *Pembroke Castle*, and when she had been launched and fitted out Sir Donald decided to arrange a cruise around Britain, starting from Barrow-in-Furness and going around Britain via the Hebrides and ending in London.

R.M.S. Pembroke Castle 1883 - 1896. 4,045 gross tons. At Dartmouth loading the mails for the Cape.

Amongst the distinguished guests on board were the Prime Minister Mr. William Gladstone and his wife and the Poet Laureate, Alfred Tennyson. At the same time as the *Pembroke Castle* was sailing through the Scottish Isles, there was a gathering of many of the crowned heads of Europe in Copenhagen. Sir

Donald, because the cruise was proving so successful, proposed an extension to the voyage to visit the coast of Norway and Copenhagen as well. All on board were delighted with the idea. When the liner reached Copenhagen the Prime Minister, Sir Donald and others were invited by the Danish King to a banquet, which was attended by many of the Royal visitors.

Shortly afterwards Sir Donald Currie invited the Royal party to visit the *Pembroke Castle* and a shortly afterwards he entertained to luncheon the King and Queen of Denmark, the Czar and Czarina of Russia, the King and Queen of Greece, the Hanoverian Royal family, the Princess of Wales and many others. After the luncheon the gentlemen were taken by Sir Donald and the Captain on a tour of the ship. The Royal ladies meanwhile went to the Smoking Room where Tennyson entertained them with readings from some of his poems. When the Royal party were about to leave the ship, the warships of a number of countries manned the yards and the National anthems of the various Royal visitors and Great Britain were played and salutes were fired. The news of this event soon reached the British newspapers and it was unfortunate that the Prime Minister had omitted to notify Queen Victoria that he was leaving the country. He wrote and apologised for the omission to which he received a rather frosty reply. Queen Victoria was not amused.

The *Pembroke Castle* was the first four masted ship of the Castle Line and she was regarded as the best looking ship in the fleet. She started out as square rigged on both the fore and the main mast. The yards though were removed when the funnel was heightened to stop the smoke blowing down on the sun deck that had been added. At the same time the Deckhouse aft for the Second Class was extended. In 1885 she was used as a troopship to the Sudan and in 1893 she was placed on the intermediate service. An early wine list of 1883 shows that the choice at that time was rather limited. Amongst the wines included were Hock and Sauterne at 3/6 Moselle (Deinhard) at 5/6. Claret was 4/- and Mumm's champagne at 7/-. No South African wines were on the list at the time, but it is likely that a limited range would have been carried.

It was at this time when trade was bad that the Union Company experimented with a new service to the U.S.A. from Liverpool to Newport News in Virginia and Baltimore. Two ships were employed on this route the *Nubian* and the *Arab*, both having previously been on the mail service. They both completed two voyages before the service was abandoned as it was making a loss. At the same time the Castle Line tried to establish a new route to Angola and the Congo but this was also unsuccessful.

It was in 1883 that unwittingly, the Castle Line became indirectly involved in the assassination of Lord Frederick Cavendish and Thomas Burke in Phoenix Park Dublin earlier in 1883. James Carey was the ringleader of the political dissidents who planned and carried out the murders. He and his colleagues were caught and stood trial for the murder of the two men. Carey turned Queen's evidence and became a witness against the other conspirators. Because of his evidence they were all found guilty and were executed. Carey now realised that he himself was likely to be assassinated. He booked a passage on the *Kinfauns Castle* to Cape Town under an assumed name. When the ship arrived he was recognised and a newspaper report leaked his real name. Patrick O'Donnell who was also Irish saw this. Carey and his family booked a passage on the *Melrose*, the Castle Line coaster to Port Elizabeth, as did his fellow Irishman. Carey and O'Donnell shared a cabin. The following day O'Donnell shot Carey three times and killed him in revenge for his act in getting his accomplices executed. O'Donnell was sent back to England on the next Castle liner to stand trial for murder. He was found guilty and was also hanged.

From 1883 President Kruger of the Transvaal Republic was interested in having a railway line built from Pretoria to Lourenco Marques. Negotiations were started with the Portuguese Government but agreement was not finally reached until 1887. Work soon started and the first shipload of materials for the new venture arrived at Delgoa Bay in April on board the *Dunbar Castle*.

In 1882 the *Arab* had been chartered by the British Government, and in company with other ships, sailed from Southampton bound for Egypt. In September of that year, as the Egyptian Army had taken control of the country, the British Navy bombarded Alexandria. Shortly afterwards the British warships and troopships arrived at Port Said and Suez and disembarked 30,000 soldiers and closed the Canal. General Wolseley was on board the *Arab* and disembarked at Ismalia. The *Arab* therefore became the first Union Line Ship to enter the Canal. At the battle of Tel-el-Kabir the Egyptian Army was defeated and British troops occupied Cairo. Again in 1885 the *Arab* was chartered to carry troops to Egypt. She subsequently became the Headquarters ship for the Naval staff at Suakin in the Sudan for the Gordon Relief Expedition. The *Conway Castle, Pembroke Castle* and *Anglian* were also used to convey troops to Suakin for this Campaign. The Army sailed down the Nile to Khartoum, taking advantage of Thomas Cook's expertise to help transport both troops and equipment. The relief Expedition arrived too late to save General Gordon and when the war was over the *Arab* conveyed Australian troops back to Sydney.

Simultaneously, there had been a 'war scare' in Britain as the Russians were on the point of invading Afghanistan. Britain gave notice that she intended to enter the war on the side of the Afghans. The Government designated sixteen passenger ships that were to be converted as armed merchant cruisers. Amongst these were the Union Company's *Mexican* and *Moor* and the Castle liner *Pembroke Castle*. Only two of these sixteen ships were actually commissioned. One was the *Oregon* of the Cunard Line and the other was the *Moor*. A further eleven of the remainder were converted but were not used, as the Russians withdrew from Afghanistan. The *Moor* was armed with six-inch guns and left Simonstown manned from the Royal Naval Reserve. She was used to patrol up and down the South African coast. At the same time Russia was in dispute with China over territorial claims and the *Mexican* was chartered to convey British troops to Hong Kong where she remained for several months until the crisis was over. The *Moor* later returned to the mail run until 1900 when she joined the intermediate service for a short period.

It was shortly afterwards that the British Government began to pay annual subsidies to Companies that agreed to make ships available when required. During the First World War forty-one liners were converted as Armed Merchant Cruisers, amongst which were the *Kildonan Castle, Armadale Castle* and the *Kinfauns Castle*.

In May 1886 a great Indian and Colonial Exhibition was opened by Queen Victoria at South Kensington, London. This brought South Africa to the attention of the British public. On the day of the opening five thousand silver leaves from the silver trees found on Lions Head at Cape Town were given away to visitors as souvenirs. On one side of the leaf was a discreet mention of the Castle Line. Shortly afterwards in Cape Town these leaves were painted, showing various Castle Line ships and were sold to visitors.

The first ships to be built specially for the intermediate service were the *Doune Castle* and the *Lismore Castle*. They were originally due to be placed on the Madagascar route. When the time came the French were not co-operative so they joined the Mauritius service instead.

S.S. Doune Castle. 1890 - 1904. 4,046 gross tons. The first Castle liner to be designed for the Intermediate service.

The *Doune Castle* made her maiden voyage in November 1890 and the *Lismore Castle* followed two months later. They both carried 150 passengers in all, of whom 30 were First Class, 40 Second Class and 80 Third Class. The *Doune Castle* was the first of the intermediates to burn Natal coal. She took on 100 tons at Durban to see if the coal was suitable and when it proved satisfactory all the intermediates started to use it. Both these ships had a fairly short career with the Company as in 1904 they were taken back by the builders in part payment for the *Cluny Castle*. The effect of the Gold Rush on the Union Line was considerable, judging by some of the advertisements in 1887 :

UNION LINE FOR THE SOUTH AFRICAN GOLDFIELDS

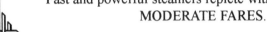

FAVOURITE ROUTE FROM THE UNITED KINGDOM
AND THE CONTINENT TO SOUTH AND EAST AFRICA
Steamers from Southampton weekly.
Fortnightly from the Continent
Fast and powerful steamers replete with every comfort.
MODERATE FARES.

An attempt to increase the quantity of homeward freight, which at the time only amounted to diamonds, gold, wool and hides, was first proposed in 1887. An experimental consignment of grapes was carried on the *Grantully Castle* in 1889 but unfortunately this was not successful. It was another three years before a shipment of peaches arrived in England in good condition on the *Drummond Castle*, which had been fitted with cool chambers. This was to be the beginning of a highly successful trade for, firstly deciduous fruit and later for citrus.

By the end of the 1880's the reliability of the engines on the ships meant that the sails were no longer considered necessary on the Union Line ships and they were withdrawn. The Castle Line retained their sails for some long time after this, well into the 1890's. The yards on the Castle line ships were also retained longer but by 1900 they had all disappeared. By 1893 the Union Line provided a guide for emigrants, which gave information about the ships both mail and intermediate. The guide stated that all the mail ships and some of the intermediates were fitted with electric light, refrigerators and cool chambers. In addition an example was given of a dinner menu for those travelling Second Class:- Soup, Roast beef and Yorkshire pudding, Boiled mutton and onion sauce, Sausage rolls, Stewed veal and peas, assorted vegetables, assorted tarts or puddings, pastry, biscuits, cheese and fruit.

In 1889 a new service was introduced by the Castle Company, and the first sailing was taken by the *Warwick Castle*. The intermediate ships leaving London would call at Flushing in Holland on their way to Cape Town. Because of this the Company was given the contract to carry the Dutch mails to the Cape. By 1890 the Castle Line was operating its own feeder service for cargo from Hamburg, Bremen and Antwerp to Southampton. In the following year the Roslin *Castle* became the last of the Currie Line ships to call at Dartmouth. They now joined the Union Line in operating the mail service from Southampton. In 1894 the Union Line began advertising round trips on their intermediates from Southampton to Hamburg, Bremen and Antwerp and back to Southampton.

In 1890 the *Tyrian* joined the Union Line fleet. She introduced a First Class coastal passenger service for the first time. She connected with the mail ship at Cape Town and had accommodation for twenty-four First Class passengers. The accommodation was considered to be the equal of the First Class on the mail ships. By 1891 she was going as far as Beira in Portuguese East Africa.

It was in the same year that the Union Line asked William Pirrie, later to become Lord Pirrie, to have a look at the harbours of East London and Durban in particular, which were suffering because of 'the Bar'. In spite of their successes with the mail ships, the Union Company at the time were losing money because they were too expensive to run. Pirrie looked at the problem and came up with shallow draft vessels that could carry cargo and a fair complement of passengers but at a slower speed of around 11 to 12 knots, than the mail ships. They had a draft shallow enough to enable them to cross the bar both at East London and Durban.

S.S. Gaul 1893 - 1905   4,045 gross tons. The first of the new 'G' class. Shown in Union Line colours.

The first to appear of the famous "G"s was the *Gaul* in 1893. She was built as an intermediate where previously most of the intermediates had been mail boats and had never drawn much public attention. The *Gaul* though, proved to be something of a 'nine day wonder' when she reached Cape Town. For one thing she was something new in her design. Her accommodation in the First Class was particularly good. She was also the first intermediate to be given a fully covered promenade deck and twin screws. She had a unique First Class dining saloon as it was on the promenade deck amidships. Previously, it was customary to have the saloon on the main deck and then it was moved to the upper deck and now a further deck higher.

The *Gaul* was very economical to run, but slow. She was designed to do the trip to Cape Town in twenty-one days, which she consistently achieved. This was the normal time for the new intermediates against the average for the mail ships of seventeen days. The design of the 'G's also made them very easy to manoeuvre, in fact they could, and sometimes did, unberth without the help of tugs. The 'G's were a great success. They attracted passengers that were not in too much of a hurry and liked, as well, to save a few pounds on the fare. It was possible by travelling Third Class in the large open men only cabin, to pay only 10 guineas. They were good sea boats and they also proved to be successful cargo carriers, just what the Union Line needed at the time. Shortly after the *Gaul*, the *Goth* then the *Greek* appeared. Next came the *Guelph*, unique in having three masts. An innovation on this ship was a First Class Lounge.

Altogether ten of this class were built between 1893 and 1900. The basic design did not change but there were some variations, particularly in tonnage. The first four to appear were between 4,700 and 4,900 gross tons and the next six were between 6,000 and 6,900 tons. Of the later ships it was almost impossible to tell the difference between the *German* and the *Galeka* but the *Galician* had been given a kind of rudimentary cross trees on the foremast, which the others never had. The *Gaika* in this class, which included the *Gascon* and the *Goorkha*, was not the luckiest of ships. She nearly came to grief at Las Palmas where she grounded when outward bound. The damage was so severe that she had to return to England for repairs. She ran as a West coast intermediate until 1913 when she was transferred to the East Africa service. She had another mishap in 1922 when she ran aground. This was in Three Anchor Bay near Green Point, Cape Town. She was soon refloated with only minor damage.

The first ship, the *Gaul* was launched in February 1893 and sailed on her maiden voyage in May. The last survivor was the *Glengorm Castle*, which originally had been named the *German*. She was taken out of service in 1930 and was broken up in Holland. The *Galician* had also been renamed and became the *Glenart Castle*.

S.S. Gascon. 1897 - 1928. 6,341 gross tons. Intermediate steamer. A later version with three masts.

Union Line Intermediate steamer Goorkha, 1897. Sister to the Gascon and Gaika.

Up until around 1890 the only steamships regularly calling at East Coast ports in Mozambique were those of the Union and Castle Lines. The first real challenge came from the Germans after they had established themselves, in what was then called German East Africa. The ships of the German East Africa Line sailed from Hamburg via the Suez Canal, calling at the ports of Tanga and Dar-es-Salaam as well as others. Soon after the gold rush started in the Transvaal, they commenced sailings via the east coast, missing out the Cape ports and calling at Delgoa Bay. The route to the goldfields from there was much shorter than from the Cape and in addition the Delgoa Bay to Pretoria railway was already under construction and was completed by 1894.

Both Union and Castle Lines had been sending coasters beyond Durban since 1875 when the *Kafir* became the first Union ship to call at Delgoa Bay. As more ports in Portuguese East Africa were added to the list, the most regular visits were made at Mozambique, Delgoa Bay, Ibo, Quelimane, Chiloane and Imhambane. The only Portuguese shipping line at the time to operate on the East coast was the "Mala Real". A service began in 1889 but by 1893 the sailings had been discontinued. The Union Line was then given a contract by the Portuguese government to send its intermediate ships to the Mozambique ports of Lourenco Marques and Beira once a month. For a time the Union Line continued this service as far as Zanzibar but they discontinued it in 1895. The port of Beira did not exist before 1891 and when the Union and Castle coasters first began to call, it was known as Pungwe Mouth. Initially the trade to Beira was small and in 1894 the Castle Company withdrew their service only to return again in 1898. When the Boer War broke out the following year the calls at Beira and Lourenco Marques were soon dropped as the intermediate ships were mainly engaged in transporting troops and military equipment.

In 1893 two separate steamer services between New York and the Cape were started. The Union and Clan Lines operated one and the Castle Line another, combining with Bucknalls. The ships sailed from New York with cargo for the Cape and Durban and sometimes might carry on to Bombay or perhaps Mauritius to load sugar. The main problem was the shortage of cargo for the return voyage to America. Mainly chartered ships were used, although in 1898 the Union Line bought three cargo ships, the *Sabine*, *Sandusky* and the *Susquehanna*. The *Sandusky* was sold within twelve months. The *Sabine* and *Susquehanna* were used mainly to carry coal from Natal to the Cape. Both Lines continued to operate, despite the difficult trade conditions and even following the merger of Union and Castle in 1900. The two American routes were to operate separately for some time. Only the *Sabine* was retained beyond a few years and she was not sold until 1921. At around the same time, the Union Line began a six weekly service from Durban up the coast as far as Mozambique.

By 1895 the new passenger ships of both companies were very different

40

from twenty years before. An contemporary account refers to the gay and beautiful saloon decorated in light yellow and gold. The chairs were upholstered in purple satin and crimson leather. The saloon was said to look like a "fairy palace".

The account goes on to say that the ship was ablaze with electric light. They had on board a very creditable orchestra made up of eight of the stewards. In the evenings there was dancing, with a cluster of six electric lights shining down on the hatch cover where the band performed. The deck around this was the ballroom. It was considered that with all the company in evening dress, there was "no prettier sight". It was so warm on some evenings that dancing went on until way past ten o'clock! There were some things that did not change for a long time. Long benches and tables in the dining saloon survived on some of the ships until they were reconditioned after the First World War. Before this the pattern of sport and entertainment on board had been established and did not vary very much over the years. Of course, in the early days some entertainments had yet to be invented. For example, the first film show ever on a ship took place on the Union liner *Norman* in 1896. It was much later than this that feature films became available to be shown on board on a regular basis. It was also only after 1919 that swimming pools and gymnasiums began to appear on the Union-Castle liners.

Passengers playing Deck Quoits and Deck Tennis on the after end of the promenade deck.

As it was said at the time, "The days on board only vary by the degree of heat. The sun is always bright and the sea is always blue". Hence the reason for referring to P. & O., Union-Castle, Royal Mail liners etc. as the 'Blue Water Liners'. The various sports competitions went on throughout the ocean voyage.

These tended to take place in the afternoon. In the morning passengers would play whist or chess or perhaps laze on deck reading or talking.

During the day passengers could play bucket quoits (rings made of rope thrown into a bucket) deck quoits (heavy discs of rubber thrown to a set of concentric circles marked out on the deck). Passengers also played deck cricket against the officers on the promenade deck with nets rigged to prevent balls going overboard. This was a game much enjoyed by touring cricket teams. There was also the daily sweepstake on the ships daily run, special children's events and in the evenings their were dances, concerts etc.

One report describes how a Fancy Fair was held on Easter Monday. This took place on deck with shooting galleries, three shies a penny and an Aunt Sally. There was even a baby show and a Father Neptune parade. The band wore, what were described as fancy costume and they played throughout. One evening would be given over to a fancy dress ball with the captain as master of ceremonies. A gold edged programme of dances would be provided for the ladies. The young gentlemen would vie with one another to fill the cards of unattached young ladies, particularly for the supper dance. A suitable cold collation would be arranged on deck together with all manner of cool drinks.

Not everyone was pleased with the entertainment now provided on the ships. Some commented that it was "unendurable". When they first travelled there was no fever of excitement and they just dawdled each day away. Even the food came in for criticism. *"We didn't eat ten or twelve courses at dinner and then quarrel with the cook because we had not had enough, thank heavens."* On the other hand many took the opposite view and were constantly asking for further improvements in standards. Even as early as 1881, the Chairman of the Union Company remarked: *"We have been educated to a standard of luxury that our forefathers never dreamt of. Even our Second Class passengers want baths, a piano in the saloon and ice at their meals."* Within seven years both Union and Castle Line steamers were equipped with refrigerators and the second-class passengers got their ice. Later still the Third Class passenger's accommodation boasted two bathrooms.

In 1890 rivalry between the two lines came to a peak. Both were building new mail ships, which were designed to outdo each other. The *Dunottar Castle* was the first to appear and sailed for the Cape in October 1890. She broke the record outward and homeward. The *Scot* sailed on her maiden voyage on 25th July 1891 and shattered the *Dunottar's* record in both directions. The *Arundel Castle* was the first of three intermediates built by the Castle line. She entered service in 1895 with the *Tintagel Castle* and *Avondale Castle* the following year.

During the 1890's both lines had suffered losses. In 1892 the Union liner *Nubian*, an intermediate ship was lost when she went ashore with a pilot on board in the river Tagus approaching Lisbon. She became a total loss.

Dunottar Castle 1891- 1913 & Arundel Castle 1894 - 1900. Alongside at Cape Town 1890's.

S.S. Avondale Castle 1897 - 1912. 5,531 gross tons. Intermediate steamer, shown leaving Cape Town in 1899.

The following year the *Durban*, also an intermediate was homeward bound with a cargo of hides and wool when she was wrecked on the island of Tenerrife near Santa Cruz. The Castle line fared no better. The *Conway Castle* had been wrecked on the coast of Madagascar on her way to Mauritius. It was ten days before the passengers who were stranded ashore were rescued by the Union ship *Arab*. Madagascar was a call for the Castle coasters at the time but in the 1880's the intermediates took over until France annexed the island. This led to the service being discontinued.

Sir Donald Currie's Company suffered by far its worst loss when the intermediate steamer *Drummond Castle* was wrecked and sank off Ushant. She was homeward bound from Lourenco Marques and left Cape Town on the 28th May 1896. She made one call at the island of Tenerrife before heading for London. It was on the 16th June that her voyage ended so tragically.

Although the sea was relatively calm as she crossed the Bay of Biscay, the weather was poor; visibility was bad and it was raining. Despite this the ship had not reduced speed, nor was the lead used. These have always been dangerous waters with very treacherous currents. Without the captain realising it the ship had gone far too close inshore. Shortly before 11p.m. the *Drummond Castle* struck a reef called Pierres Vertes. Four minutes later all that remained of the vessel was floating wreckage. There had been no time to launch any of the boats.

It was around nine o'clock the following morning that some fishermen picked up two seamen who had been clinging to a hatch cover. In addition one passenger was also picked up by a fishing boat and was landed at Ushant. Out of the 245 people on board the ship these were the only survivors.

Mr. Marquardt, the surviving passenger cabled the Castle Company in London from Ushant with the news that the ship was a total loss. When word of the disaster broke in London the Castle Line offices in Fenchurch Street were besieged with relatives and friends seeking news of those that had been on board. It became necessary to bring in special constables to control the traffic.

In South Africa people were stunned when they got news of the catastrophe via the telegraph. The whole country went into mourning and even the Parliament in Cape Town was adjourned as a mark of respect. In St. George's Cathedral in Cape Town their are two memorials to the sinking of the *Drummond Castle*. One was sent from Southampton and was placed in the crypt. Also the pulpit is dedicated to the 242 persons who lost their lives in this terrible disaster.

It is strange how long it was before the First Class accommodation on the Castle Line ships was moved from the stern to amidships. It was far more comfortable when the ship was pitching and there was less chance of soot and smuts blowing down on the deck further forward. The first intermediates of the

Castle Line to feature the changes did not appear until the 1890's. The trend for the new ships of the nineties was really set by the Union Line when the *Norman* appeared in 1894.It was during this period that South Africa began to be a holiday destination for the wealthy classes. A problem for those travelling to the Cape and thence up country was the standard of the hotels. Even Cape Town attracted many uncomplimentary comments. In one case the City hotels were described as both 'mean and dirty'. One writer suggested that the shipping companies themselves should do something about this situation. Sir Donald Currie was aware of the problem and it was not long afterwards that the Castle Company decided to build its own hotel. It purchased the Mount Nelson estate, which was at the top of the Government Gardens very handily placed in relation to the City. Sir Donald's son-in-law, Mr. F.J. Mirrielees was in charge of the new venture and it was very quickly decided that the name Mount Nelson should be retained for the new hotel. The manager was to be Swiss and also Swiss staff was to be employed. On March 4th 1899 an inaugural luncheon was held and two days later the hotel opened its doors.

It was in 1895 that both the Union and Castle Lines discontinued their services to Knysna. Calls had started in the late 1880's when gold was discovered near Millwood in the hills close to the town. Both Lines called regularly, the Union Line with the *Saxon* of 470 tons and the *Natal* (618 tons), and the Castle Line with the *Venice* of just over 500 tons. The gold rush·that was anticipated never happened and the ships were withdrawn.

A Union Line pamphlet of 1898 makes interesting reading. It lists all the vessels in the fleet at the time and gives information on the intermediate steamers which reads as follows:-

Intermediates are despatched from Hamburg fortnightly, calling at Rotterdam and Antwerp alternately, and sail from Southampton every alternate Saturday, taking passengers and goods for South and East African ports without transshipment. The intermediate steamers call at the Canary Islands and make a regular service between Germany, Belgium and South Africa.

Passengers are conveyed to: Madeira and the Canary Islands, and passengers and goods to St. Helena, Ascension, Cape Town, Mossel Bay, Port Elizabeth (Algoa Bay), East London, Natal, Delgoa Bay (Lourenco Marques), Inhambane, Beira (Pungwe River), Zambesi, Quillamane, Mozambique and Zanzibar. The call at Zambesi would have been at the small port of Chinde. Passengers for Nyasaland (Malawi) disembarked here and were then transferred to houseboats. These were towed up the Zambesi and then the Shire River for about two hundred miles to Port Herald, which was close to the Capital Blantyre. This continued until the 1920's when the Beira/Blantyre railway was completed. The basket for lowering passengers onto the tender was also used here.

This notice goes on to advise passengers that the liners carried both a

Surgeon and stewardesses and that they also had electric light and refrigerators.

By 1899 the new Victoria Basin in Cape Town was just about complete as the threat of war between Great Britain and the independent states of Transvaal and Orange Free State became a certainty, The Alfred Dock, completed in 1870 had been considered too small for some long time. Trade had increased and so had the size of the ships. The dock was only ten acres in area and the outer basin a mere four acres. The breakwater extended to 1870 feet. Some improvements had been carried out over the years and in 1876 work on what was to be called the Robinson Dry Dock had been started and this was opened in 1882. The first ship to make use of it was the Union liner *Athenian* of 3,877 tons. Later, the *Norman* also of the Union Line became the largest ship (7,537 tons and drawing twenty two feet) to use the new dock. She had suffered damage to a propeller. Also in 1883 the Time and Tide Gauge House, better known as the clock tower was completed. This was also the Port Captain's office. He would often be seen on the quayside with his megaphone directing proceedings as the ships passed through the entrance into the dock.

It had been in 1883 that Sir John Coode first submitted his proposal for an outer harbour. This would add 64 acres of enclosed area and around 5,000 feet of extra quayage. Nothing happened for a number of years as the proposal coincided with the beginning of a trade recession. Things began to change though in 1886 when gold was discovered in the Transvaal and work at last began in 1889. The breakwater was completed within two years and was now 3,640 feet long. To build this breakwater it had taken two million tons of stone. In 1893 the Loch jetty was also completed and the South pier and elbow were finished just as the Boer War broke out. Very soon the new harbour could not cope with the numbers of ships bringing troops and supplies. On one day 128 ships were counted within the harbour and lying off in Table Bay.

Sir Donald Currie was always seeking publicity for the Castle Line. He decided on another cruise for the opening of the Kiel Canal by Kaiser Wilhelm 11. This was bound to attract a great deal of attention and publicity. The *Tantallon Castle* was the ship chosen and Mr. William Gladstone and his wife were to be the principal guests again. The ship sailed from London with a hundred guests on board, initially for Hamburg. From there she cruised to Copenhagen where the Danish Royal family were entertained on board to lunch. At Kiel the guests watched as the canal was opened by the Kaiser. The Press in England gave the event and the *Tantallon Castle* a great deal of publicity.

In 1894 the time-ball, the bright red ball on top of the Dock House tower was brought into use at Cape Town docks. This was invented in 1829 when it was seen as a revolutionary means where for the first time, longitude could be accurately measured. The ball was dropped at a given time so that ship's captains could adjust their chronometers to give them accurate measurements.

The first time-ball in Cape Town had been at Observatory and later this was moved to Signal Hill. However because the city was growing it had become harder to see the time-ball from the sea. This was why the new time-ball was placed on top of the tower which stood on the ridge overlooking the harbour.

On the 11th October 1899 the 2nd Boer war broke out. Within a fortnight 109 ships had been requisitioned as troop Transports. Of these fifteen were from the Union and Castle Lines. They were the *Gascon, Goorkha, Gaika, Mexican, German, Moor, Kildonan Castle, Kinfauns Castle, Harlech Castle, Lismore Castle, Hawarden Castle, Roslin Castle* and *Braemar Castle*. The *Trojan* and *Spartan* were converted as hospital ships. Later other Company ships were commandeered including the *Goth, Greek, Guelph*, and *Tintagel Castle*. The final total of ships requisitioned was in excess of 200.

In December 1899 the Union and Castle Lines agreed to merge under the name of 'The Union-Castle Mail Steamship Company Limited' and on the eighth of March 1900 the new Company came into being, only a few months after the Boer War broke out.

CHAPTER 3 - AMALGAMATION AND EXPANSION

When the new mail contract was awarded jointly to the Union and Castle Lines, the clause that had previously stopped the merger of the two companies had been left out. It was then that Sir Donald Currie suggested an amalgamation of the two Lines to the Union Company. They accepted this in December 1899. The new Company was to be called - The Union-Castle Mail Steamship Company Limited. It was also decided that the colours of the Castle Line should be adopted for the combined fleet. These were red funnel with a black top, white upperworks and lavender hull. The new house flag was a clever combination of both Lines original flags. In February 1900 the amalgamation of the two lines took place. Southampton became the base for the mail ships, and all the intermediates used the East India Dock. So numerous were the Company ships using the East India Dock that they were known locally among the longshoremen as the 'Blackwall Navy'. There were in fact twenty intermediates at that time, ten from each Company. They were all employed during the Boer war and it was not until 1904 that the numbers began to be reduced. During this period though it was not uncommon for six or more of the ships to be berthed alongside each other at Blackwall.

Meanwhile the Boer war had commenced in October 1899. This meant that the flow of troops and munitions to Cape Town from England disrupted the intermediate services although the mail service was hardly affected. The first ship to reach the Cape with reinforcements was the *Roslin Castle* but she was sent on to Durban where the troops were needed to halt the Boer advance in Natal. Within a few days of the *Roslin Castle's* arrival at the Cape, she was followed by the *Lismore Castle* and the *Harlech Castle* with more troops on board. The mail ship *Briton* was also requisitioned at the outbreak of war for one voyage only. She carried 1,500 troops to Cape Town. Hardly a mail ship left the U.K. without nurses, volunteers, stores etc. on board. Many other ships from P. & O, Royal Mail, Cunard, British India and other Companies were requisitioned and they had to be altered to carry the large numbers of troops, field guns and other military stores.

The new *Kildonan Castle* that was just about to join the mail service, was quickly altered and sailed a fortnight later packed with a total of three thousand troops on board. It was believed at the time that this was the largest number of people ever carried on one ship. She was not designed to carry such a large number, which did create some problems, one of which was that water had to be rationed. In addition it was difficult to continue with normal military training in such cramped conditions.

In the Boer republics, once the war seemed inevitable, both Union and Castle Line offices in Johannesburg were overwhelmed by miners and others who wanted to get back to Great Britain and other European countries.

The Union-Castle staffs themselves were forced to leave in early October 1899 to go to Cape Town. By December nearly 15,000 people had taken passage from the Cape to England mainly on the new Company's intermediate vessels.

R.M.S. Kildonan Castle. 1899 - 1931. 9,652 gross tons. Arriving in Table Bay with 3,000 troops on board.

Once the war had actually started, many more people fled from the Transvaal and the Orange Free State to the coast. As they could not get to Durban or Cape Town, they travelled through Portuguese East Africa to Lourenco Marques. One of the ships that was due to pick up refugees was the *Avondale Castle*, but she failed to arrive. As she approached Delgoa Bay she was stopped by H.M.S.*Partridge* and arrested. She had on board a shipment of gold for the Transvaal, and although she had clearance for this shipment, she was not allowed to proceed, and she had no alternative but to return to Durban. Eventually the British government compensated the Union-Castle Line but as a result the service to Lourenco Marques was halted for a year. In addition to most of the intermediates being converted to troopships, the *Trojan* and *Spartan* were requisitioned at Southampton in October 1899 and were fitted out as hospital ships. They were Britain's first true hospital ships with the P & O's *Egypt*, the *Orcana* of the Pacific Steam Navigation Company and the *Maine* of the Atlantic Transport Line. All of these were chartered for the duration of the war. The *Spartan* was used mostly to transfer wounded from Durban to the base hospital at Cape Town. Later, the *Lismore Castle* was added.

Because of the war, coal production in Natal was halted due to the advancing Boer forces. By this time Union-Castle were using large quantities of this coal on their intermediate ships. It meant that additional alternative supplies had to be brought out from the United Kingdom, mostly by sailing ships. It was not long before the docks at Cape Town were unable to cope with all the war materials and other supplies that were pouring in. By early in March 1900 complete chaos existed in Table Bay, with a mass of shipping waiting to discharge cargo. The problems that existed at Cape Town were duplicated in the ports up the coast.

The build up of British troops sent to South Africa once the war had started was rapid. The figures for troops (Officers and men.) sent to the Cape for the first six months were as follows:-

October	1899	28,703
November		29,174
December		19,763
January	1900	27,854
February		33,591
March		27,348

The total for the six months was 166, 277. This meant that there were few days in the month when a troop transport did not arrive in Table Bay with perhaps 1,000 soldiers on board with all their arms and equipment. It is no wonder that the port became very congested.

The *Dunottar Castle* was the first to fly the new Union-Castle flag, on 17th March 1900, when a special ceremony was held shortly before she was due to sail for the Cape from Southampton. As the flag was broken at the masthead, it was also raised on the intermediate steamer *Gaika* which was berthed astern of the *Dunottar Castle*. The *Gaika*, crowded with troops on their way to South Africa, sailed first and as she passed the *Dunottar Castle* the soldiers cheered the flagship to the echo.

It was during this period that the Company lost one of its mail ships, the *Mexican*, which was sunk in collision with another vessel. With the merger of the two companies this did not disrupt the mail service at the time. However, when a year later the *Tantallon Castle* was wrecked on Robben Island, despite the combined efforts of the *Avondale Castle*, *Raglan Castle* and the *Braemar Castle* to tow her off, the Company was short of a mail ship. They then decided that the remaining mail vessels would either turn around at East London or Port Elizabeth. First of all the *Pembroke Castle* provided a shuttle service between these ports and Durban and then, later she was replaced by the *Arundel Castle*.

The congestion at the docks in Cape Town was seriously affecting the war effort and the problems were no better further up the coast. To try and speed up the process of unloading, the Company sent out three small craft from the United Kingdom. They were the *Lochgair* and *Machrie* that both went to Port Elizabeth, and the *Bellona*, a steam lighter that had her own winch. She worked initially in Port Elizabeth and then in Table Bay, with other lighters that had been shipped out from England and then assembled on arrival. The passenger tender *Natal* from Durban was also sent to Table Bay. This was because most of the intermediates had to lie off in Table Bay as there were no berths available for them to go alongside. The *Natal* operated a shuttle service between these ships and the docks, ferrying both passengers and cargo.

The *Kildonan Castle* operated as a troopship for over twelve months, carrying many thousands of soldiers to Cape Town. In December 1900 she was given a fresh assignment. She was sent to Simonstown where she took on board some 2,500 Boer prisoners of war who had been kept in very poor quarters. The transformation to this new environment was a vast improvement on the conditions they had suffered ashore and they soon settled in on board. Some six weeks later though the *Kildonan Castle* had to return to Cape Town and the prisoners were transferred to two other transports.

An illustrated record of a voyage on the troopship The *Tintagel Castle* was made on board the ship. She sailed from Southampton en route to Cape Town at 2.45 p.m. on the 10th March 1900. She was carrying 1,200 troops together with a small number of passengers. At the time it was thought that a record of such a voyage would be of interest to the public and on return to England it was printed by the Government printers and published.

S.S. Tintagel Castle 1896 - 1912. 5,531 gross tons. Intermediate steamer converted to a troopship in the Boer War.

The two people responsible for compiling this record were the ship's surgeon, Dr.W.McLean and the third officer E.H.Shackleton. He was later to be knighted for his exploits as a Polar explorer, particularly as Commander of the Nimrod Expedition to Antarctica of 1907 – 1909 and his famous boat journey of 1914 – 1916.

The *Tintagel Castle* was an intermediate steamer of 5,531 gross tons. She could maintain a regular speed of 13½ knots and could carry in normal conditions 6,000 tons of cargo and 500 passengers in three classes. For a trooping voyage, clearing some of the cargo holds made extra space. The messing arrangements were considered by those with previous experience of trooping to be excellent. A constant supply of fresh drinking water was available on each deck. On the upper deck washhouses were situated which permitted 36 men to wash at a time. All the troop decks had electric light. On the main troop deck for example there were 20 lamps that gave a good light for reading.

The Armoury was situated forward where 1,200 rifles and sword bayonets were rested in large racks. On the deck below some six hundred tons of Lyddite, (a powerful explosive composed mainly of Picric acid) plus shrapnel shell and small arms ammunition were stowed.

Understandably no smoking was allowed except on the upper deck and even then only at stated times. The hospital was on the upper deck and contained thirty-five beds and a dispensary. Daily at 10 a.m. all who were sick were seen by the Medical Officer in charge, the ship's surgeon and a civil surgeon assisting.

The troops had one canteen forward and one aft where they could buy beer or mineral waters. The food was cooked in the galleys on the upper deck, and nearby were the vegetable locker and the Baker's and Butcher's shops. The saloon in which the military and ship's officers messed, was right amidships on the upper deck, whilst the cabins occupied by them were on the upper promenade and main decks. The crew numbered 123 all told so that in total there were well over 1,300 people on board.

The only port of call en route to Cape Town was Las Palmas. Soon after arrival coaling commenced and this went on for several hours. The soldiers were able to buy fruit, tobacco and cigars from the numerous bumboats that swarmed alongside the ship. After a stay of eight hours the *Tintagel Castle* left Las Palmas passing the troopship *Fifeshire* also on her way to the Cape.

For the troops the day began at 5.30 p.m. when hammocks were stowed and the men then washed, brushed their clothes etc with drill at 7.30 when breakfast commenced. After a hearty meal the days work began: some at target practice off the stern, others cleaning rifles in the Armoury etc. The sick attended Hospital at 10 a.m. and at 10.30 there was assembly, when all who had no other duties paraded on deck. Down below decks, tables etc were scrubbed and special attention was given to the cleaning of washhouses and toilets. At 11a.m. the Colonel and his staff carried out a thorough inspection of the Mess Decks, hospital, washhouses etc. Each day a regiment took it in turn to furnish guard.

Entertainment for all, occupied part of the day. The Crossing the Line Ceremony took place with Captain Harris welcoming Neptune on board. A makeshift pool was rigged and some of the troops were questioned then lathered by the barber before being ducked. Forty officers, troops and passengers went through the ceremony. At the end an unexpected visitor appeared. It was none other than Kruger who had been discovered on board. He was dragged before the court wearing a slouch hat' a rope beard and a pipe. This was a poorly disguised 3rd Officer Ernest Shackleton. The court dealt with him before being hurled into the pool.

Obstacle races were also held and there was also the sweep on the ships daily run. To keep fit there was doubling around the deck-nineteen laps to the mile with the temperature at 88 degrees F. Passengers could take advantage of the various deck games, quoits etc.

The troops had no complaint about the food provided on board. In fact the catering was far beyond their normal fare. A typical days menu was: Breakfast comprising of porridge and Golden syrup, stewed steak, bread and butter and coffee, Dinner was soup, roast beef, boiled mutton, cabbage, boiled potatoes, compote of figs, tea and cold meats and pickles, jam, tea and bread and butter. Supper was bread, cheese and biscuits.

Abreast of Cape Verde the *Tintagel Castle* passed the *Scot* on her way to Southampton. She signalled the news of the occupation of Bloemfontein the capital of the Orange Free State. A few days later the *Dunvegan Castle* passed during the night and the steam whistle blew a greeting and the troops responded with a cheer. As the ship neared Cape Town the intermediate *Arundel Castle* passed homeward bound. On arrival the ship anchored in Table Bay on the 31st March 1900. The troops did not disembark until the following day. The total time for the voyage was 20days, 6 hours and 39 minutes and the distance travelled was 5,953 miles

While the war was in progress, all the Union-Castle Liners came from the United Kingdom crammed to capacity with both passengers and cargo. The voyage back was a different matter. There was little cargo to be carried because of the disruption caused by the war

Early in 1902 the *Dunvegan Castle* was coming in to Cape Town and on entering the basin, hit the end of the elbow making an enormous hole in the stonework yet scarcely damaging the ship. This was not the Pilot's fault. The ship was arriving late, which was a habit of hers, and the Captain was in a hurry to come in. The flag was in his favour but just as the ship was about to enter, the Military authorities, who were in control of the harbour , pulled down the flag to allow another ship, the *Cilicia* to undock. The Captain of the *Dunvegan*

Castle was a short-tempered man, and he refused to be dictated to and kept on his way. However, to avoid a head on collision with the other vessel, he ported his helm and hit the elbow. The harbour board estimated the damage done at £10,000. It is not clear who actually footed the bill for the repairs.

R.M.S. Dunvegan Castle, 1896 - 1923. 5,958 gross tons. Taken off the mail run in 1904. Made some Summer cruises and was then laid up for a time.

The war finally ended on the last day of May 1902. Soon the troopships began to return the British soldiers to England. Altogether half a million troops had been engaged in the conflict. Of these 20,000 were killed and 80,000 injured. It was Britain's most expensive war as it cost some 200 million pounds. By this time the new *Walmer Castle* had joined the mail fleet and a normal service was fairly quickly restored. The intermediate services took longer to restore, as so many had been converted to carry troops and now had to be reconverted to carry passengers again. Another change was that all the intermediate service ships would now use the East India Dock at Blackwall in London. These ships operated a regular service, first to Hamburg, Rotterdam and Antwerp, before returning to London to take on passengers and more cargo bound for South & South West Africa, Mozambique and Mauritius.

Towards the end of the war, in anticipation of a boom, the Company built new ships and bought others. Four of these were the *York Castle, Gordon Castle, Corfe Castle* and *Aros Castle*. They were mainly used on the South Africa - U.S.A. - U.K. route. The Company also built what were described as extra steamers suitable for carrying large numbers of emigrants. The first two to appear were the *Alnwick Castle* and the *Berwick Castle* of just over 5,900 tons. The following two, the *Cawdor Castle* and *Newark Castle* were slightly larger at just over 6,200 tons. They all had much the same passenger accommodation with twenty in the First Class, twenty in the Second Class and five hundred in Third Class. Finally, two further extra steamers appeared in 1903, the *Cluny* Castle and the *Comrie Castle* at around 5,100 tons. These steamers were also used on the Mauritius run calling at Lobito Bay and occasionally at Mossamedes in Brazil.

The expected boom never materialised and at one time the Company had fifteen ships laid up. It was 1905 before all the ships that were no longer required had been sold. It was interesting that when all the surplus vessels had been disposed of or scrapped there were still fifteen intermediates left. All ten of the 'G' class ships from the Union Company were retained but only three from the Castle Line plus two more that had been built since the merger.

After the war was over King Edward VII presented a silver Transport Medal to officers of the Merchant navy who had been engaged in the transport of military personnel and equipment to and from South Africa. Twenty-six of these medals were awarded to Union-Castle officers.

It had become the practice, about 1896, to carry bananas from the Canary Islands back to London on the ships of the intermediate service. This helped to make the fruit popular in England. By 1899 the *Braemar Castle* carried 2,000 tons from Las Palmas on one voyage, a record shipment at the time. After the Boer war the *Machrie*, which had been used in Port Elizabeth, was sent to Santa Cruz in Teneriffe, where she was operated by a Spanish crew, carrying bananas from Puerto de la Cruz on La Palma to Santa Cruz and transhipping the fruit to an intermediate ship on her way to London. Eventually, because she was not a Spanish owned vessel, she had to be withdrawn and sold.

By this time there was a more extensive wine list carried on the ships. A selection of items included:- Sherry, pale Dry 3/6 a bottle, Burgundy, Claret and Hock all at 4/-, champagne Moet & Chandon, dry Imperial, Heidsecks dry Monopole, Perrier Jouet Cuvee all at 10/-. Cape wines are included all at 2/- a bottle for sherry, Pontiac, Hermitage and Drakenstein (Hock). Spirits were 6d per glass with Scotch whisky 3/6 per bottle, Brandy 4/-, Gin and Rum 2/6.

The *Braemar Castle* probably had the most varied career of any Union-Castle vessel. She was laid down in 1898 at the Glasgow yard of Barclay, Curle & Company. She was the last ship in the fleet to be given four masts but she had no yards on the foremast from the beginning. She joined the intermediate service in March 1900 where she remained for a time before becoming a troopship. On her first trooping voyage she carried a detachment of the Royal Service Corps to Cape Town. In 1902 she ran aground on the Isle of Wight but was refloated, having suffered only minor damage.

When the war came to an end the *Braemar Castle* was once more hired as a troop transport by the British government and was used mainly for transferring troops to and from the Far East and she was given a yellow funnel and a white hull with a blue stripe. She had another short spell as an intermediate before the First World War. Then, she again became a troopship, initially carrying the British Expeditionary Force to France. In 1915 she went to Gallipoli with a battalion of Royal Marines. She was then commissioned as a hospital ship to which the hospital transports brought the sick and wounded. In 1916 she was mined in the Aegean and was towed to Malta for repairs. Because of delays, after three months she was towed again to La Spezia in Italy where she was finally repaired.

Russia, despite the efforts of the Allies to keep her in the war, signed a separate peace with Germany in February 1917. At this time in Archangel there were huge supplies of all sorts of military stores and equipment that had been sent to Russia by the Allies. The Germans wanted to get hold of these supplies and turn Murmansk into a submarine base. To try and stop this, British troops were sent to Murmansk at the beginning of 1918. The *Braemar Castle* was sent as the base hospital ship. She was there for a year and at one time, because of the severe weather she was boarded over to keep out the cold. As a result she became known as "Noah's Ark". At one point Sir Ernest Shackleton, the Antarctic explorer, who had at one time been a deck officer with the Union-Castle Line, visited her. He had joined the Company in 1899 when he became 4th officer on the *Tantallon Castle*. He then moved to the *Tintagel Castle*. By October 1900 he had become 3rd officer on the *Gaika*, earning the princely sum of £8 a month. The last Company Ship he was on was the *Carisbrook Castle*, also as 3rd Officer.

On one trooping voyage the *Braemar Castle* called first at Southampton on 1st January 1910, and then called at Gibraltar briefly before sailing to Bermuda. She left there on the 20th January and called at the island of St.Vincent where she embarked the 2nd Battalion Duke of Cornwall light infantry. After a call at the Cape Verde islands she sailed for Cape Town arriving on the 12th February where she disembarked the troops. On this voyage she steamed 10,512 miles. At this time a Deck boy was paid £1 a month, the ship's cook £4 and the Chief Engineer £22.

In 1920 the *Braemar Castle* reverted back to being an intermediate once again. The following year though she was back in Archangel evacuating the sick and wounded. She reverted once more to the intermediate service before being requisitioned and trooped to both India and China. In 1922 she was back in the Aegean because of the conflict in Turkey. Finally in 1924 she was scrapped.

Because of the tight schedules that Union-Castle maintained with their passenger liners, it was rarely possible to find time to slot in cruises, even for a day. Early on, as mentioned previously, because the mail ships were in Table Bay for approximately a month, they used such trips as a means of advertising the new Company. They also, at around the same time, did something similar with trips around the Isle of Wight from Southampton. A little later the Castle Line also took invited guests for trips down the river Thames.

Much later, in 1904 when the *Dunvegan Castle* was placed in reserve, she was used for cruising with paying customers. She did a number of cruises to the Mediterranean, the Norwegian Fjords and around Britain, whilst the *Dunottar Castle* was laid up and was later chartered for a passenger service from New York to Panama. Later on, in 1909 Sir Henry Lunn's Travel Company chartered her and she also made a number of cruises, mainly to Norway. These cruises went on in the summer season for three years. In November 1911 she took a group that included some Members of Parliament to the Great Durbar in Delhi.

The basket trick - Starting off

The old method of landing people = how would you like to have your xmas bath, by being dropped into the ocean in one of these

The basket trick at East London, showing how the Passengers embarked and disembarked at some Cape Ports.

An entirely new design for the intermediate ships appeared in 1904. These were the 'D' class vessels, all of which were 8,200 tons. They were the *Durham Castle, Dover Castle* and *Dunluce Castle*. They only carried First Class and Third Class passengers and soon became very popular. This was due in some part to the improvements made in the Third Class. The Dining room had revolving chairs and also there was now a smoking room and a Ladies Lounge. The cabins were for two, four or six persons and baths were now provided. In addition the Third Class had a library, a piano and electric lights.

R.M.S. DUNOTTAR CASTLE IN NORWAY.
The Cruising Co., Ltd., 5, Endsleigh Gardens, Euston,

R.M.S. Dunottar Castle 1891 - 1913. 5,625 gross tons. Cruising to Norway in 1908.

S.S. Dunluce Castle, 1904-1939. 8,114 gross tons. Built for the intermediate service. Took the first sailing to Mombasa via the Cape.

58

On March 18th 1904, the *Berwick Castle* was en route from Southampton to Hamburg when she was involved in a disastrous collision. She was off the Nab lightship when she rammed and sank the British submarine A1. All those on board the submarine lost their lives in the accident. The submarine was one of a new class that were being developed for the Royal Navy. They were a mere one hundred feet in length and were petrol driven. The accident happened when the submarine appeared to stop and then suddenly surged forward into the path of the *Berwick Castle*. The A1 was one of fourteen of her class that had been built and her sinking led to questions being asked in Parliament.

In 1905 there were new developments in the Portuguese colony of Angola on the West coast of Africa. A survey had been made in June for the new Benguela railway and later that year the *Gascon* arrived at Lobito Bay with the engineers and equipment to start work. Once this large project was underway, considerable quantities of railway track and other supplies were brought in by sea. This led to Lobito Bay becoming a regular port of call for the Union-Castle intermediate ships. They were already calling at Walvis Bay, which was a detached part of the Cape Colony at that time. The call here was usually on the homeward run.

By 1906 the extra steamers were calling quite often at Beira on their way to Mauritius. Three years later, when they started to build the railway to Northern Rhodesia and the Copper belt, the *York Castle* brought in the first 4,000-ton shipment of rails.

The *Newark Castle* left Durban for Mauritius calling at Lourenco Marques on the 12th March 1908. She had on board a crew of sixty-nine and forty eight passengers, mostly soldiers for the Mauritius garrison. About 5.45 p.m. on the same day, when some three miles from the shore, she struck a rock not far from the mouth of the Umhlatuzi river, near Port Dunford in Zululand. She was obviously badly damaged and the water level was rising in the engine room and the Captain decided to abandon the ship. The boats were launched and everyone taken off within twenty minutes. The ship remained afloat and as darkness fell the order was given to stay together and make for the shore. Three of the boats remained near the ship and during the night the third officer reboarded the *Newark Castle* and fired off a series of distress rockets. The steam trawler *Evelyn* saw these. She made for the scene and at daylight saw the wreck and took off those on board. They soon found three of the boats, which left one missing. About 1.p.m. a party was seen on the shore. The Captain and some of the crew went back on board the *Newark Castle* while the trawler set off for Durban with the decks crowded with passengers. They arrived safely in Durban some 16 hours later. It was learned shortly afterwards that all in the party that reached the shore had not survived as three people had drowned in the surf, which swamped the boat. The rough seas floated the ship off but she then blew ashore on to a sandbank seven miles away and became a total loss.

In 1908 the Union-Castle Line decided to operate day cruises to Simonstown from Table Bay, using the intermediate steamers. This was to become a great event in the South African holiday season and the first ship, the *Goorkha*, was full to capacity with five hundred passengers. She cast off at ten o'clock in the morning and steamed down the coast past Seapoint and Camps Bay towards Cape Point where lunch was served. Soon afterwards the ship reached Simonstown. The passengers then returned to Cape Town on the train. The inclusive price of this outing; for lunch, the landing charges at Simonstown and the rail fare back to Cape Town, was twelve shillings and sixpence a head. Little wonder that the *Galeka* was well filled when she repeated the excursion a little later and finally, a third voyage by the *Galician* was organised in March.

These voyages became a regular feature of the Cape holiday season for a few years, Then, in the early summer of 1910 the new liner the *Grantully Castle* set off with hundreds of trippers on board. When they got to Cape Point a gale force South-easter blew up and when the ship arrived at Simonstown the Captain would not let the passengers land as he considered it too dangerous. Passengers not only received lunch, but also dinner and slept comfortably for the night, some in First Class cabins. In the morning the gale had subsided and the tugs landed everyone at the pier to catch the train. This was the last of such cruises because of the uncertainty of the weather. On this occassion the *Grantully Castle* was late sailing from Cape Town on her voyage up the coast. It had become a rather costly cruise for the Company.

Sir Donald Currie died in 1909 at Sidmouth in Devon. His health had been failing for some months. His son-in-law, Frederick Mirrielees who was later to be knighted, took his place.

In 1910 the self-governing colonies of Natal, Cape Colony, Transvaal and Orange Free State formed the Union of South Africa. The first parliament of the new Dominion was opened by the Duke of Connaught at Cape Town in November of that year. It was originally intended that the Prince of Wales would open this first parliament but he had succeeded to the throne as King George V on the death of King Edward V11. The *Balmoral Castle* was chosen to serve as the Royal Yacht to carry the Duke to South Africa for the opening. The previous September she was taken out of service so that changes to the accommodation could be made and she was also to be repainted. The funnels were to be yellow as were the masts and derricks. Apart from a few members of the original crew she was manned by the Royal Navy with Commodore Wemyss in command.

By this time the fruit export trade from South Africa had grown considerably following the first successful shipment in 1892. The season for deciduous fruit was from December to June, and by 1910 nearly 200,000 packages of fruit were being exported annually. In addition shipments of citrus fruit, principally oranges, had also begun and over 10,000 packages were despatched in that year. The main deciduous fruits being shipped were grapes, peaches, pears and plums. Other fruit like apples were being exported but only in small quantities. The season for citrus fruit is from May to October and this meant that shipments of fruit were now being exported mainly to Britain for around ten months of the year.

In the August of 1910 the *Balmoral Castle* did some short·cruises. They were round the Isle of Wight carrying invited guests of the Company. She made three cruises and on one of these Marconi was on board and guests could send messages on the new wireless telegraphy equipment. All the mail ships were carrying the new equipment by January 1911 and by the end of that year the intermediates had the equipment as well.

With all the Union-Castle ships carrying the new wireless, it was not long before wireless stations were opened in South Africa. One was at Cape Town and the other was on the Bluff at Durban. In 1912 Donald Currie and Company retired from the management of the Line and the Royal Mail Group of Companies were successful in taking over the Union-Castle Company. Lord Kylsant (then Sir Owen Phillips) became Chairman and Managing Director. It meant that the Group now became the largest shipping company in the world. Union - Castle however, still continued to operate exactly as before.

Advertisement circa 1911-12. Shows the fleet list, fares and destinations. The liner shown is the Norman.

During the decade after the Boer War ended, the Company had been keeping a close watch on developments on the East coast. At the time the intermediate service went no further than Delgoa Bay on a regular basis. Developments were also beginning to take place with the railways in East Africa. By 1901 in British East Africa, the line from Mombasa to Uganda had been completed. In German East Africa the line from Dar-es-Salaam to Lake Tanganyika had been started in 1905. Also in Dar-es-Salaam a small dockyard had been built and in general port facilities were improving. In addition, with the development of the railway from Beira to the Rhodesias and the export of copper ore as a result, Beira became a regular port of call for Union-Castle.

In 1909 the passenger liner *Waratah*, en route from Australia to London had left Durban with over 200 people on board. She should have called at Cape Town three days later, but she never arrived. Months passed and still nothing was heard of the ship. No wreckage was found and it was as though she had just vanished. The intermediate steamer *Guelph*, was perhaps the last ship to sight the *Waratah*. Early in the morning of the 27th July a large vessel was sighted in heavy seas off Hood's Point. The officer of the watch called her up by using a signal lamp to try to identify her. The reply could not be fully read but the last two letters were 'AH'. All sorts of theories were put forward as to what might have happened. She certainly had run into bad weather on leaving Durban and there were suggestions that she was top heavy and may have just turned over. Another possible problem might have been her wooden hatch covers, which may have been smashed in, causing the vessel to sink. Neither of these suggestions really explained the lack of wreckage. The Australian government decided that a search should be made southward of the normal shipping routes. The view was that the *Waratah* might have drifted and without radio would not have been able to communicate what had happened. They chartered the Union-Castle cargo vessel *Sabine*. She was fitted out with towing gear and searchlights and ample provisions in case they discovered the missing liner. On the 11th September she left Cape Town with instructions to search southward in an area of about 3,000 square miles. She also had no radio and was not seen again until the 7th December when she was sighted approaching Table Bay. When she anchored the authorities went on board only to find that the *Sabine* had found no trace of the missing liner. To this day the disappearance of the *Waratah* remains one of the great mysteries of the high seas. It is even stranger that apparently there have been four ships with this name between 1848 and 1909 and all were lost without any trace. More recently, Clive Kussler, the author of "Raise the Titanic" has instigated a lengthy search for the *Waratah* and thinks she is lying in 117 metres of water off the mouth of the river Xora, which is to the north-east of East London. Other experts dispute this theory but with the developments in underwater search techniques it is possible that we may have an answer to this mystery in the not too distant future. Further searches have since been made and it now appears that this is indeed the *Waratah*. Perhaps now it will be possible to find out why the ship sank without trace.

One of the main problems that the Company had on the East coast was that they could not compete with the German East Africa Line because they were provided with a subsidy from their government. The British government though were not prepared to give Union Castle a similar subsidy, which meant that most of the freight and passengers to and from British East Africa were carried by the German line. This included the Royal Mail, Colonial Civil servants and even British troops. They dominated the trade on the East coast and other Lines like Union-Castle could not compete. British India tried to operate a direct service from England but that had failed in 1892. The Austrian Lloyd Line lasted for a period but withdrew their cargo liners in 1906. None the less in 1909 the Company decided to extend the intermediate service to Mombasa, still without a subsidy.

By now the information booklet for passengers was extensive. Advice was given as to the clothing required both on the voyage and in South Africa: '*The only outfit that a passenger to the Cape really needs is some warm clothing for the Channel and commencement of the voyage, and some of a lighter texture to wear after Madeira is passed. English summer or yachting clothes are perfectly suitable for the latter purpose. sufficient linen etc. to last the whole voyage should be taken. English summer clothing of light texture and colour is also that which is most generally worn in the towns of South Africa and special clothes need only be provided by those who have decided to proceed into the interior, where clothing of a material not easily torn is necessary. In a question such as outfit, which depends so entirely on individual tastes and habits, it is impossible to give advice.*'

The new service to Mombasa started in January 1910 and the *Dunluce Castle* took the first sailing from London via the Cape. Sailings were at monthly intervals and the *Dover Castle* and *Durham Castle* were employed on this route. The new service was immediately successful despite the competition from the German East Africa Line. Agreement was finally reached with the British government over the proposed route from London to Mombasa via the Suez Canal. There was still no subsidy but outward freight and passengers that were under the control of the Colonial Office would be carried on the Union-Castle liners. In addition support would be given for the transport of freight from British East Africa. The first sailing on what was called the Royal East African Service was taken by the *Guelph* on the 14th September 1910. This also was a monthly service, which carried on down the East Coast to Durban and then returned back to London via the Suez Canal. The other vessels used on this route were the *Goth*, *Goorkha* and *Gascon*. In 1912 the *Guelph* and *Goth* were transferred to Royal Mail, because of passenger complaints about the standard of the accommodation. They were replaced by the *Dunvegan Castle* and the *Carisbrook Castle*. These ships linked up with the mail boats and other intermediates at Durban and, as passengers transferred from one ship to another, so the Round Africa voyage by Union-Castle became possible. It was because of the opening up of the East Coast that the Company dropped the Second Class. It meant that the Third Class was now far superior to anything that had been provided previously. The accommodation now included a smoking room a ladies' lounge, baths and a library. In terms of what had gone before this was indeed luxury. In all, ten new intermediates were built in the period leading up to the First World War.

Following the success of the 'D' class ships the Company had built five more intermediates between 1910 and 1911. The first two were the *Grantully Castle* and the *Garth Castle*, both just under 4,800 tons. The latter three were slightly bigger at 5,900 tons. These were the *Galway Castle, Gloucester Castle* and the *Guildford Castle*. Capable of 13 knots they were a knot slower than the 'D' class ships and were never quite as popular.

UNION-CASTLE LINE TO SOUTH AND EAST AFRICA.

INTERMEDIATE STEAMER "GLOUCESTER CASTLE."   7,999 TONS.

S.S. Gloucester Castle, 1911 - 1942. 7,999 gross tons. Intermediate steamer, initially on the West coast route.

During the period from 1911 until the outbreak of the war in 1914, on sailing days from Southampton, the Captain and deck officers of the Line wore Melton cloth frock coats. These were similar to those worn by officers of the Royal Navy. After the ships departure these smart uniforms were put away and not worn again until the next sailing day from Southampton. On the day of departure there would be a crew inspection and boat drill prior to the arrival of the boat train from Waterloo at eleven o'clock. This brought not only the passengers but also the managers and departmental heads from the London office of the Company. A magnificent luncheon, supervised by the ship's chef would be served at noon. A selection of items from the extensive menu would include:- Hamble crab, lobsters, raised game pie, pheasants in flight, capercailzie, (largest of the game birds from Scotland weighing up to twelve pounds) Royal baron of beef, lamb cutlets etc etc.

By 1911 the Company was advertising:

PLEASURE TOURS AND HOLIDAY TRIPS
TO MADEIRA AND THE CANARY ISLANDS.
From April to September ocean return tickets
are issued at the reduced rates of eighteen
guineas First Class, twelve guineas, Second Class.
FROM LONDON TO HAMBURG, ANTWERP AND BACK.
Including accommodation and meals on board while at sea and in port.
First Class fare: Eight guineas.
Duration of round voyage about 9 days.
TO SPAIN AND THE MEDITERRANEAN.
The sailings to and from the Mediterranean
of the steamers engaged in the Company's Royal
East African Service afford opportunities for
pleasure tours at moderate fares. Full particulars
can be obtained on application.
TOURS ROUND AFRICA.
Passengers can make the tour of Africa in Union-Castle Line steamers,
going out via the East Coast and returning via the West coast or vice versa,
transhipping at Natal.
Ocean fares from: 74 guineas First Class.
Duration of voyage about 64 days.
MOUNT NELSON HOTEL, CAPE TOWN.
The premier hotel in the Colony. Inclusive terms can be arranged from
15/- per day, according to position of room and length of stay.
Cuisine and cellar unexcelled.
Fifteen minutes drive from the Steamer Quay.

In the period leading up to the First World War the intermediate service was weekly, leaving London on Friday and Southampton on Saturday. Extra services called at Lobito Bay, the coast ports and Mauritius and operated four weekly. In addition there were regular sailings by extra and intermediate vessels between London/Antwerp/Rotterdam and Hamburg. A steamer was also despatched regularly from London and Southampton via Gibraltar, Marseilles, Naples, Port Said and the Suez Canal to Port Sudan, Aden,

Mombasa, Zanzibar, Mozambique, Chinde, Beira, Lourenco Marques and Durban, returning to England by the same route. Passengers could travel overland and join the ship in Marseilles or Naples and could therefore leave London a week later than the sailing date of the steamer. The voyage thence to Mombasa occupying about seventeen or eighteen days. The sailings of these steamers was arranged to connect at Durban with the Royal Mail steamships for the return voyage to Southampton. Passengers joining the East Coast steamers in London would embark in the East India Dock Basin, close to Blackwall station. Trains left Fenchurch Street station (Great Eastern Railway) for Blackwall about every twenty minutes. Passengers joining the steamer at Southampton would leave Waterloo by special train on the day of sailing. The special trains ran alongside the steamers in Southampton Docks.

UNION-CASTLE LINER SIGNALLING "ALL'S WELL."

In 1912 new ships were ordered for the East Coast service. They were of an entirely new design and at over 11,300 tons, were much larger than previous vessels. In fact they would be larger than three of the current mail ships. The standard of accommodation was also better than some of the older mail boats and they were to be the first Union-Castle liners to have a passenger lift. The two ships were to be given Welsh names reflecting the new Chairman's Welsh origins. (*see facing page*)

Also in 1912 the new Mail contract provided for the free conveyance of horses, cattle, sheep, and pigs from the United Kingdom to the South African ports. The animals were looked after during the voyage by experienced cattlemen and several thousand

R.M.S. Balmoral Castle. 1910 - 1939. 13,361 gross tons. She is signalling 'All's Well' to another Union-Castle vessel.

animals were carried free of freight charges. This resulted in a great improvement in the stock of the farming community throughout South Africa and Rhodesia.

In March 1914, the *Dover Castle*, shortly before entering Port Elizabeth harbour struck Roman Rock. She made port and anchored off the North Pier with nineteen feet of water in the forehold. Passengers were disembarked and were transferred to the *Galway Castle* to carry on their voyage up the coast. She had 109 passengers on board at the time.

In 1914 the Union-Castle made a unique move for the time in producing advertising stickers to go on the back of envelopes. These were triangular in shape, reminiscent of the early Cape triangular stamps. They were perforated and at a glance they could have been mistaken for rather colourful postage stamps. There were eight different views. Union-Castle ships, Ports of call, and interiors of the ships. They were much larger than the original Cape triangulars and were multi-coloured. Very few of these seem to have survived, probably because they were issued just prior to the outbreak of the First World War.

In March 1914 the *Llandovery Castle* arrived in Mombasa on her maiden voyage. Many excursions from up country were organised so that people could visit the new intermediate ship. The Press reports at the time were almost lyrical in their praise for the new ship. In one case she was described as "A veritable floating palace." The First Class dining saloon was unique in that it occupied the whole width of the ship with portholes on either side. Another change was in the layout. The long tables with swivel chairs had been abandoned and had been replaced with small square and round tables scattered here and there. The saloon was decorated in white and gold, which reminded one journalist of a Parisian restaurant. The chairs were no longer fixed to the deck, but could be moved freely. The lounge and library were decorated in Georgian style and the cabins were spacious. With the adoption of the Bibby system, all the cabins had portholes. Another first was the inclusion of a laundry, which must have been welcomed by the passengers and the ship's company. The ship's laundry was also dealt with on board and not accumulated on the long ocean voyage. A mail ship could arrive back in Southampton with not far short of 100,000 pieces of soiled linen. Soon afterwards the *Llanstephan Castle*, the sister ship of the *Llandovery Castle* sailed on her maiden voyage. She was also received with acclaim. Alike in all the main features, the ships only differed in the style of decoration. They were without doubt the finest ships seen on the East Coast and thousands flocked on board to see them at the various ports. The *Llandovery Castle* on her way back to London met up with the *Llanstephan Castle* in Mombasa. This meeting of the two ships was referred to as the "gathering of the *Llans*." The *Llandovery Castle* and *Llanstephan Castle* were built at different yards and were not exactly the same although they were always spoken of as sister ships. The *Llanstephan* was slightly the smaller and her gross tonnage was 11,348 whereas the *Llandovery* was 11,423 gross tons. At the time they were larger vessels than the mail ships *Briton, Kinfauns Castle* and *Kildonan Castle*, and far more up to date.

In the three months that preceded the outbreak of war it became the practice to offer special excursion fares on the coast. This involved both the mail ships and the intermediates, as with the latter these special excursion fares applied to both Delgoa Bay and Beira as well. The return fare for example from Durban to Beira was eight guineas and to Delgoa Bay four guineas. The intermediate steamers involved, included the *Gaika* and *Gascon*, the *Braemar Castle, Carisbrooke Castle, Dover Castle* and *Dunluce Castle*, the last two being on the Royal East African service.

A lot of the Union-Castle publicity at the time, was focused on the facilities offered on both the mail and intermediate ships. One brochure makes interesting reading and illustrates how many improvements had occurred since the turn of the century. It refers to: *"the Drawing, Reading and Smoking rooms are well equipped with writing and card tables and a liberal supply of magazines, papers etc. is put on board. On most of the steamers a piano and an organ will be found in the First Class, while pianos are also provided in the Second and Third Class for use at concerts, dances and fancy dress balls. An orchestral band is provided on all the Royal Mail steamers and also on some of the intermediates."*

"There are good libraries for the use of first, second and Third Class passengers on board. Chess, draughts and other games are also supplied. There are hairdressing saloons on all the mail ships and on most of the intermediates.

"The cabins are arranged to meet the needs of all passengers and there are single berthed rooms, rooms for two, and a number of family cabins. Some are fitted with double beds and some with communicating doors. Most of the First Class cabins are fitted with chests-of-drawers or Wardrobes, and everything is calculated to add to the comfort of the passenger during the voyage. In the Third Class, cabins containing two, four, and six berths are provided in most steamers. The question of ventilation has received careful study and a complete system, in excess of the requirements of the Board of Trade, has been adopted, electric fans being largely utilised in many of the Company's steamers in addition."

At the beginning of 1914 it was intended to operate a regular monthly sailing by the intermediate steamers to Mauritius. Leaving London they would call at the French port of Boulogne, hoping to attract cargo and passengers as the vessels would call at the island of Reunion. The ships to be used were the *Gloucester Castle, Galway Castle, Grantully Castle* and *Guildford Castle*. The last named took the first sailing in 1914 but again because of the war the service was terminated after just the one sailing.

CHAPTER 4 - THE GREAT WAR

When the first World War broke out in 1914 Southampton became a closed port and only those ships controlled by the Admiralty could enter it. It was from here that the majority of the first British expeditionary Force was conveyed to France. The *Norman* and the *Dunvegan Castle*, which had been in reserve, took part in this operation. The *Carisbrook Castle*, also in reserve, was the first Union-Castle liner to be converted to a hospital ship. Another was the *Garth Castle* that became attached to the Grand Fleet and served at Scapa Flow, Cromarty Firth, and the Firth of Forth, apart from a short period when she was sent to Malta. In February 1915 King George V visited her when he was inspecting the fleet.

Following the landings in France on the 9th October, six of the Company's liners embarked a total of 6,000 troops and all their equipment, which then sailed for Egypt.

Back in the Cape at the outbreak of war, there were still some 4,000 British troops. Six Union-Castle liners were used to ship them, their families and equipment back to England never to return. Three of the intermediate steamers were used in this famous convoy, which left Table Bay on the 27th August 1914. They were the *Goorkha, Dunluce Castle* and *Guildford Castle* together with three mail ships *Balmoral Castle, Briton* and *Kenilworth Castle*. The Naval escort ships were the cruisers *H.M.S.Hyacinth* and *H.M.S. Astrea.*

Southampton was ideally placed to be the Number one military port for shipping troops to the front in France. The majority of the British merchant fleet was requisitioned by the government for the duration of the war. Union-Castle had forty-three ships and immediately prior to the war, dispatched two ships a week from England to South and East Africa. Out of that forty-three, at one point the Company were left with only three cargo boats to try to maintain the regular services. Some were converted as armed merchant cruisers, others became troopships or hospital ships, or just carried munitions and supplies.

At the very beginning of the conflict no one really appreciated what a gigantic task it was going to be to transport armies, munitions and stores to the various fronts. In 1914 the United Kingdom owned around half of the world's merchant shipping amounting to 20,000,000 tons. When the end came about half that tonnage, 9,000,000 tons had been lost. During the war though, some 5 million tons had been added. New ships had been built and others captured.

Immediately the war commenced a considerable number of liners were fitted out as armed merchant cruisers. The *Armadale Castle* was at Southampton on the 4th of August and within a week she had been converted and allocated to the 10th Cruiser squadron. The *Kinfauns Castle* when she arrived, first of all disembarked her passengers and mail and once her cargo was discharged, the work of converting her began.

*R.M.S. Norman in dry dock at Cape Town. 1894 -1926. 7,537 gross tons.
The first Company liner to be requisitioned as a troopship in 1914*

*The convoy to England which carried the British garrison of 4,000 men
from Cape Town on the 27th August 1914.*

Fittings had to be removed and also any inflammable materials; Cabins on the main deck were gutted. Everything that made the ship vulnerable when under attack was also removed. Finally eight 4.7" guns were mounted, four on the forward deck and four aft. Because of their importance, both the engine room and the bridge were specially protected. Magazines were built in some of the holds with the lifting tackle needed for hoisting up the ammunition. In addition to all this, searchlights had to be fitted, stores and ammunition loaded. The *Kinfauns Castle* sailed on the 15th August. Later on the *Edinburgh Castle* and the *Kildonan Castle* were also commissioned as armed merchant cruisers.

At the beginning of the war the biggest danger to shipping came from mines and surface raiders. The threat from submarines came much later on. Several of these armed raiders were at sea very quickly after war was declared. Some of them were pre-war liners that had been converted but in addition there were some German navy cruisers at large, like the *Emden* and the *Königsberg.*

Early in the war the South African government decided that an attack should be mounted on German South West Africa. Two of the intermediate ships were chartered to act as troopships. They were the *Galway Castle* and the *Gaika.* The invasion fleet left Cape Town on the 15th September 1914 escorted by the *Kinfauns Castle* and the *Armadale Castle.* Landings took place and the town of Swakopmund was occupied. However in October because of problems in South Africa and a German naval force operating in the South Atlantic, plans were halted for the time being. It was not until some six months later when the German fleet had been sunk at the Battle of the Falklands that the landings in South West Africa recommenced. By the 9th July 1915 the German forces surrendered and the campaign came to an end.

On one trooping voyage the *Gaika* left Tilbury Docks and proceeded down the English Channel to Plymouth. She then joined a convoy on what turned out to be a nine-week voyage to Cape Town. When she left the convoy she sailed well out into the Atlantic towards Brazil before turning east and heading for West Africa. The ship put in at Bathurst (now Banjul), Gambia, Senegal, Freetown, Sierra Leone, Accra, Gold Coast (Ghana) Sekondi, (Takoradi) also Ghana and finally Lagos, Nigeria, embarking native levies en route. On occasion the *Gaika* had to slow down to enable her naval escort, *H.M.S. Astrea* to catch up! She eventually arrived in Cape Town some 63 days after she left Tilbury. In 1916 she was still employed as a troop transport on the East Coast. Later in 1917 she was placed on the run to Australia.

Neither the *Llanstephan Castle* nor the *Llandovery Castle* were requisitioned immediately by the Government, although later in 1916 the *Llandovery Castle* was converted to a hospital ship. The *Llanstephan Castle* was also requisitioned in 1917. Early in 1915 she was en route to Zanzibar when she was ordered to return instead to Durban. This was because the German raider *Konigsberg* was known to be in the vicinity of Zanzibar.

The campaign in German East Africa was much more protracted. Indeed General Von Lettow Vorbeck only surrendered several days after the Armistice was signed on the 11th November 1918. This tiny army of never much more than a thousand fighting men plus porters and camp followers, defied the Allied armies of much greater numbers for the entire length of the war. Amongst the troopships used on this campaign from 1916 until the end of the war were the *Cluny Castle* and the *Comrie Castle*.

In the first weeks of the war nineteen Union-Castle ships had been requisitioned. This meant that the intermediate services were severely affected and the sailings via the Suez Canal had been suspended. The *Gascon* was the first ship to sail from England in August 1914 and she was carrying the mails for South Africa. Leaving Cape Town she then set off up the East coast heading for Mombasa. She was due to call at Zanzibar, but as she approached the anchorage early in the morning, those on board could hear the sound of heavy guns firing. The *Gascon* immediately turned tail and sailed on to Mombasa. She had just missed the German cruiser *Königsberg* that had arrived at Zanzibar and was shelling the cruiser *H.M.S. Pegasus* from Simonstown. She was an old ship and a sitting target, she was no match for the more modern *Königsberg*. The *Pegasus* had been ordered to clean boilers in an open roadstead. Her Captain pointed out the danger. He was told that the ship had to take her chance. After a short engagement the *Pegasus* was sunk.

Later, the *Gascon* returned from Mombasa, converted as a hospital ship. She then took the survivors of the battle back to Simonstown. The *Gascon* remained as a hospital ship and spent the rest of the war in the African theatre.

Following the sinking of the *Pegasus*, the hunt for the *Königsberg* was intensified. British naval ships were involved and also the armed merchant cruiser *Kinfauns Castle*. The *Königsberg* had sailed from her base at Dar-es-Salaam and had gone north to the Gulf of Aden where she sank the Ellerman Line ship the *City of Winchester*. Meanwhile *H.M.S. Astrea* had shelled Dar-es-Salaam and destroyed the wireless station. In addition the German forces sank a floating dock at the entrance to the lagoon at Dar-es-Salaam to stop British Naval ships entering. It did of course also mean that the *Königsberg* could not return to her base. She then hid in a creek in the Rufiji delta at Salale. The British Navy was aware of roughly where she was hidden but it was necessary to pinpoint her exact position. The *Kinfauns Castle* returned to Durban to take on board a small aircraft and the pilot. They put the plane ashore at Niororo Island where the plane took off from the beach and after a short search was able to pin point the position of the *Königsberg* some distance up the Rufiji River. The British warships did not have guns with a long enough range to reach her from the open sea. Two monitors, the *Mersey* and the *Severn* were sent out from England, and when they arrived, destroyed the *Königsberg* with their long-range weapons. After scuttling the ship the crew of the *Königsberg* abandoned her, taking with them anything of use and joined the tiny German army of General Von Lettow Vorbeck.

The _Galician_ had a lucky escape in the early days of the war. She was returning to London when the German raider, _S.M.S. Kaiser Wilhelm der Grosse_, intercepted her near the Canary Islands. She had been a liner of the Nord-Deutscher Lloyd line on the North Atlantic run. She was a very well known ship and at one time had held the Blue Riband for the North Atlantic crossing. Having stopped the _Galician_ she sent a boarding party across which destroyed her wireless so that she could not send any messages. After interrogating the Captain, two military passengers on the liner were taken off the ship as prisoners of war. The boarding party returned to the German raider taking with them some medical supplies. Those left on board the _Galician_ thought that the ship was about to be sunk because they were told to swing out the lifeboats ready for lowering and to bring their belongings on deck. In the end though, the German captain changed his mind because there were women and children on board. She was allowed to continue on her way to London. Shortly afterwards the _Kaiser Wilhelm der Grosse_ was sunk. _H.M.S. Highflyer_ found her when she was coaling and sank her with shellfire off the African coast on the 16th August 1914. She had been painted all in black but this did not disguise her well-known outline with four funnels. Her sinking came less than two weeks after the war started, so her career as a raider was very brief. When the _Galician_ arrived in England she was renamed _Glenart Castle_. At the same time the _German_ was also renamed and she became the _Glengorm Castle_.

The Union-Line coaster _Ipu_ was one of the few Company vessels that continued more or less as before the war began carrying cargo and passengers up and down the East Coast. A letter written in June 1916 by one of the deck officers on board gives some idea of the trials and tribulations of wartime voyages. He apologises in the letter to his girl friend back in England whom he hoped to see in October when he was relieved: -

_'I am afraid this will be a very disjointed letter but you see I am supposed to be on duty so I have to look down every hatch every few minutes to see if the cargo is being stowed properly. When we arrived here (Beira) it was decided to sail next Wednesday or Thursday but the owner of large sugar estates up the Zambezi river, and a shipper of some importance to Union-Castle is waiting to go to Chinde and has asked to leave tomorrow, so to please him the manager agreed. The result is that everything is a horrible rush. We started discharging cargo at six this morning and must work until one or two a.m. without any break. We can then rest until six a.m. when the work starts again and continues until we leave at 4 p.m. We cannot rest then as the Chief and I must keep four hour watches tomorrow night while at sea...

Why did I ever go to sea! If I get a chance I shall not forget to tell this millionaire what trouble we have been put to. Do you remember me telling you_ that Mr. Hamilton was a 1st class passenger on the *Walmer Castle* and he came with me on the *Umvoli* and then was passenger to Chinde on his way to Zumbo. Well, his wife came out also on the *Walmer* and arrived at Durban on the 30th May. She will have to wait there until June 12th for a steamer, then when she arrives here on Thursday we shall be at Quelimane and so she must stay here until we come back. Even then she may have to stay for another week or so because there will be no cargo for us to take to Chinde. The cheapest hotel is 15/6 a day so she will have an enormous bill to foot. She is alone and I am supposed to meet her, but cannot, so she will not know what to do.'

At the beginning of the war British merchant ships were painted grey unless they were hospital ships. These had to be painted in the designated colour, white and have large red crosses displayed, which could be illuminated at night. They were protected under the Geneva Convention but as the war progressed this proctection proved less than successful. The allies needed new measures to stop the sinking of ships carrying vital supplies. It was in 1917 that the well-known marine artist, Norman Wilkinson, who was serving in the navy, came forward with new ideas how best to camouflage merchant vessels. Wilkinson accepted that it was virtually impossible to make ships invisible. The only thing you could do was to break up the ships outline to make identification more difficult. As this was not strictly camouflage, it was initially called dazzle painting, and later disruptive patterns. A dazzle section was established under the supervision of Norman Wilkinson and many artists became involved. First of all fifty troopships were painted, with designs to suit each ship. Soon the other allies took up the idea and it was applied to some naval vessels too. The Union-Castle ships the *Balmoral Castle* and the *Walmer Castle* were amongst the earliest to be painted. The latter in fact is recorded as having two distinctive patterns at different times. It was proved at the end of the war that there was less chance of being sunk by submarines if the ship was dazzle painted.

The Company's first loss was the *Galeka*, towards the end of 1916. She struck a mine and went aground on rocks near Le Havre. There were no patients on board at the time but the initial explosion killed nineteen members of the Royal Army Medical Corps. Salvage work went on for some time but she eventually became a total wreck. Not long after this, at the beginning of 1917, the war at sea intensified and submarines began to play an increasingly important part.

The Dunluce Castle had been converted at the beginning of the war to a troopship but in 1915 she became a hospital ship and was sent initially to the East African theatre. In February 1917 she was stopped by a U boat and inspected to check that she was complying with the Hague convention. She was then allowed to proceed. This is believed to be the only occasion that such an inspection occurred. The *Grantully Castle* was another intermediate ship that was converted to a hospital ship as were a considerable number of the intermediate ships. It appears that their size and design made them eminently suitable for this work. Of the seventeen intermediates in the fleet no less than fourteen were converted to hospital ships plus two mail ships, the *Kildonan Castle* and the *Dunvegan Castle*, the latter had been in reserve. In all there were seventy-nine hospital ships requisitioned, of which sixteen were Union-Castle. Between April and September 1915 nearly 100,000 sick and wounded were evacuated from Gallipoli, mostly to Egypt.

S.S. Dunluce Castle was originally converted to a troopship, but in 1915 became a hospital ship.

The *Grantully Castle* was also involved in the Dardanelles campaign. While she was there, the poet Rupert Brooke was brought on board. He was transferred to a French hospital ship and was taken to the Greek island of Skyros where he later died. He was buried on the island, in an olive grove above a watercourse at the foot of Mount Khokilas. Seven other Union-Castle hospital ships were involved at Gallipoli, namely the *Braemar Castle*, *Dunluce Castle*, *Galeka*, *Gascon*, *Gloucester Castle*, *Goorkha* and *Guildford Castle*.

The conditions on these hospital ships were not always up to standard. The *Galeka* on one voyage sailed from Gallipoli bound for Malta with wounded soldiers. By some administrative error the *Galeka* was allocated more passengers than she was able to accommodate. This resulted in a hundred V.A.D.S.(Voluntary Aid Detachment) having to occupy two big wards in the hold which previously had been used by convalescent soldiers suffering from dysentery and all sorts of other ailments. The beds were swinging iron cots

S.S. Grantully Castle. 1910 - 1939. 7,612 gross tons. Became a hospital ship in 1915. Seen here anchored off Salonika.

S.S. Galeka was the first Company ship to be sunk towards the end of 1916.

R.M.S. Kildonan Castle 1899 - 1931.9,664 gross tons. Was converted to an armed merchant cruiser in 1916.

made up with blankets and mattresses used previously by the sick. 'The conditions were appalling and many V.A.D.'s went down suffering from headaches and acute diarrhoea. Sixteen fell ill on one day alone. Food poisoning was diagnosed once the ship reached Malta and the *Galeka* and *Brittanic* were both detained for several days while both ships were disinfected.

In March 1917, for three months the Union-Castle Line had taken over the job of stevedoring munitions in the Southampton Docks. In that time the Company was responsible for loading 610 ships with horses, artillery, lorries and other vehicles etc. Altogether it came to just below half a million tons of war materials. Throughout the war, the port of Southampton was stretched to the utmost to cope with the men and materials passing through. Taking the Union-Castle hospital ships alone during the period of the war they disembarked some 354,000 wounded officers and men who had come mostly from France but also from the Mediterranean and as far afield as the Persian Gulf.

Also in March 1917 the extra steamer *Alnwick Castle* was torpedoed 320 miles west south west of the Scilly Isles. The previous day she had picked up 25 of the crew of the *Trevose* that had been sunk. She then had a total of 139 people on board. The ship began to sink rapidly by the head and the six boats were lowered and all on board got safely into them. While they waited for the ship to sink the U boat surfaced close by and remained there silent until the *Alnwick Castle* went down. The submarine then submerged and left the scene.

Of the boats, two were never seen again as they had become separated because of the bad weather. Four of the boats were eventually picked up but many of the occupants had died because of the conditions. Amongst the ninety-nine survivors were a mother and her small baby. The *Glenart Castle*, originally the *Galician*, had a narrow escape in 1916. She arrived in the vicinity of Cape Matapan where several submarines had been operating. She picked up 476 survivors from two ships, the *Welsh Prince* and the *Lundy* both of which had been torpedoed. She was considered to be a lucky ship as she was stationary for some long time in this very dangerous area. She had previously served as a hospital ship at Gallipoli and then later in the Indian Ocean and the Mediterranean. In 1917 she struck a mine between Le Havre and Southampton. At the time she had 520 sick and wounded patients on board all of whom were transferred to destroyers and other ships in under an hour. She was then towed into Portsmouth and repaired. In February 1918 her luck ran out when she was torpedoed in the Bristol Channel on her way to Brest where she was to have evacuated Portuguese sick and wounded. She sank in five minutes and out of a total on board of 206 only 38 survived,

During the course of the war many of the Company's ships found themselves travelling into waters that they would not normally have visited. The *Kildonan Castle* sailed from Oban in Scotland under sealed orders early in 1917. Here she had embarked the Anglo/French Mission that was bound for Russia. This was the second attempt, as the first mission ended in disaster. This was when the cruiser *H.M.S. Hampshire* had been sunk with Lord Kitchener amongst others on board. The situation at the time was causing the Allies concern. The passengers on board the *Kildonan* Castle were to make an attempt to keep the Czarist government from making a separate peace with Germany. The party numbered thirty and included, from the British side, Viscount Milner and General Sir Henry Wilson, and from the French, Monsieur Domergue, later to become the President of France, and General de Castenau. The *Kildonan Castle* and her escorts took five days to reach Murmansk where the members of the mission left the ship for St.Petersburg. The ship waited for their return. It was intensely cold and icebreakers had to free the ship from the ice several times. It was uncomfortable for those on board, as the Union-Castle liners were not built to withstand these conditions. When the members of the mission returned the ship sailed back to Scapa Flow. In the autumn of 1917 the new Soviet Government went ahead and signed a separate treaty with Germany.

The sinking of the *Llandovery Castle* on the 27th June 1918 was the worst disaster of all for the Company. She had on board 258 people of whom 94 were medical officers and nurses. She was fully lit up showing her Red Cross lights when she was torpedoed south west of the Fastnet Rock bound for Liverpool. Those that survived got away in the boats, but the *Llandovery Castle* was gone inside ten minutes. The submarine responsible for torpedoing her surfaced and shelled the boats. Only one boat containing the Captain and 23 other survivors was rescued. After the war the Commander of the submarine and one of his officers were both tried as war criminals and sentenced to four years imprisonment. However within a few months both had escaped.

Also in 1917 two other Company hospital ships were torpedoed. The first was the *Gloucester Castle* where all but one on board were saved but three patients died while being transferred to another vessel. The ship eventually reached port to be repaired. The *Dover Castle* was torpedoed without warning in the Mediterranean but all on board including 632 patients were rescued.

After the South West African campaign the *Galway Castle* had returned to commercial service. In October 1917 she ran aground on Orient Beach, East London but with the aid of tugs and a high tide she was floated off a few days later. The following year she became the last Company ship to be sunk. She left Plymouth on the 10th September 1918 bound for Cape Town. She had on board a crew of 204 plus some naval ratings, 346 civilian passengers mostly in the Third Class and approaching 400 invalid South African troops, some of whom were blind. There were in total almost a thousand people on the ship. For the first thirty-six hours she was in convoy and then the ships were dispersed and went their separate ways. The following morning the *Galway Castle* was torpedoed 200 miles from Lands End. There was a heavy sea running but they managed to launch eighteen of the twenty-one boats despite the fact that 'the ship had broken her back. Also forty life rafts were put over the side. Within an hour all had left the ship with the exception of the Captain and about forty volunteers from the crew. These were taken off by another ship just before she went down. Of the near 1,000 that were on the ship 857 survived.

When the war was over the *Kildonan Castle* was retained as a troopship and went to Northern Russia, India and the Near East. Following this she sailed from Newcastle to Vladivostock via Far Eastern ports to bring back 1,800 Yugoslavs who had been chased or forced to trek right across Russia to Siberia. The *Kildonan Castle* picked them up and took them to Gravosa in the Adriatic.

A number of enemy ships that had been captured were handed over to Union-Castle during the course of the war to manage on behalf of the government. One of these was the *Polglass Castle*. The *Polglass Castle* survived the war and was sold in 1921. The *Leasowe Castle* was built for a Greek company by Cammell Laird of Birkenhead. When she was completed she was placed under Union-Castle management and became a troopship operated on the run between Marseilles and Alexandria. She was an unlucky ship. She was torpedoed off Gibraltar on 20th April 1918 but made port and was repaired. About five weeks later, when she was back again on the same run she was torpedoed once more whilst in convoy North west of Alexandria. She had on board 2,900 men of the Warwickshire Yeomanry plus the crew. She sank in an hour and a half with 92 lives lost. The Captain was convinced that had the ship remained afloat for another five minutes all would have been saved.

The *Huntscliff* was another ship that was managed by Union-Castle. She was originally the *Rufidji* of the German East Africa Line. Early in the war she was captured and in 1916 she was handed over to Union-Castle. She became a troop transport and was used initially in the East African campaign.

By the autumn of 1918 the *Huntscliff* was in Montreal waiting to be loaded with a full cargo of grain and oil. The grain was loaded in bulk, as bags were unobtainable. It was recognised at the time that this was risky if she encountered bad weather, which was highly likely at this time of year.

She left in convoy with other vessels escorted by *H.M.S. Tuetonic* on the 29th September. The weather for the first few days was fine. However, on the 5th October a heavy westerly gale was encountered. The *Huntscliff* hove to and she started to list to port. During the night though the weather improved and the convoy got underway again. The Chief Engineer trimmed the ship upright by moving coal and water from bunkers and tanks.

The following day the weather worsened again. The ship rolled heavily and listed ten degrees to port. The vessel again hove to. All hands then began to shift the grain but the list still increased. By 8p.m. the list was twenty-five degrees and more. The crew continued to work the cargo but the list was ever increasing. By early morning on October 7th the list was thirty-five degrees but all hands continued to shift cargo. The Captain was still hoping to save the ship. Later the senior officer, realising that he would have to proceed shortly with the remainder of the convoy, signalled the *Huntscliff* as to whether the Captain wished to abandon ship or wait for tugs and escorts to arrive. The Captain did not wish to abandon the ship. The work of jettisoning cargo continued through the night. Later, water began to come up through the hatches and the list steadily increased.

The next morning the wind and sea were rising and the list was now dangerous and the *Huntscliff's* crew were transferred to the *Teutonic*. The Captain had called for volunteers to remain with him but the men regarded the position of the ship as hopeless. The Captain therefore also decided to leave the ship.

The weary crew had a good nights rest. The heavy weather continued until October 12th when it began to moderate. On the same day an American tug *Jenesee* arrived on the scene. The Captain, officers and members of the crew managed to get back on board the *Huntscliff* and they commenced at once to clear away the starboard anchor and cable for connecting the towline. At 11a.m a signal from the *Teutonic* ordered them all to leave the ship. A submarine was in the area and the *Teutonic* and the tug would have to steam away from the danger.

The following day a tug and two sloops arrived and a five-inch hawser was at last connected with the tug. This soon carried away and was replaced with a six-inch hawser. At 7 p.m. the tow commenced. That night and through the next day, October 15th the ship moved eastwards at a speed of five knots. In the early hours of the next day the wind rose again and the position of the ship was critical. The situation on board was soon hopeless and by 5.30 a.m. the list had reached forty degrees. All hands were transferred into boats and they were picked up by the *Tuetonic*. The *Huntscliff* soon began to sink by the head. The ship had been towed 280 miles and she foundered only 120 miles from her destination, Bantry Bay. It was a gallant endeavour which deserved to succeed.

When the Armistice was signed in November 1918 Union-Castle had lost eight ships from the pre-war fleet. Six were passenger liners but strangely none of the mail ships were lost. In addition the *Aros Castle* and *Carlisle Castle*, both cargo ships were also sunk by German submarines. The Company's losses were far fewer than many other lines. The Clan Line for example had lost close to half of their fleet.

CHAPTER 5 - BETWEEN THE WARS

Only five ships were available to Union-Castle at the end of 1918 to resume the normal commercial services. Two intermediate ships, the *Llanstephan Castle* and the *Durham Castle*, which were employed on the mail service, together with three of the cargo vessels, *Berwick Castle*, *Cawdor Castle* and *Chepstow Castle*. Within twelve months though, sufficient ships had been refitted for peacetime service and so some of the normal sailings were restored.

Some months after the war had ended, the *Durham Castle* was still on the mail run when an unfortunate incident occurred. She was in Cape Town, due to sail for Southampton with the leader of the South African Opposition, General J.M.B.Hertzog and his staff, on board. He was on his way to England to have discussions with the British government about South African independence. The General had been a supporter of the 1914 Dutch rising in South Africa. The crew on the ship refused to sail with the General and his supporters on board. There was a stalemate for some time but eventually the crew changed their minds and the ship sailed for England with General Herzog and his party.

It was in 1922, that the intermediate service was fully resumed. Instead of leaving from London and calling at Southampton weekly, they now sailed fortnightly from London. Once a month a call was made at Plymouth to embark passengers. At this time the Union-Castle intermediate vessels were among the largest ships to go up the river Thames to dock in the Blackwall Basin in the East India docks on the Isle of Dogs. This was not far from the Pool of London, which stretches some two miles from Wapping to Southwark. Later the intermediate service was based on the South West India Dock and the ships used the landing stage at Tilbury to embark and disembark passengers. However, occasionally, if the liners were due to arrive or sail at night because of the tide, then passengers would board or disembark at the docks. Many of the Company's ships were retained by the government for a long time, in particular the intermediate vessels. It was necessary of course to repatriate all the troops that had been in Europe. For example to Australia, Nigeria, New Zealand, Canada, India, South Africa and many other countries. Sometimes troops returning home tended to be rather high-spirited. On one voyage the *Guildford Castle* was taking South African troops back to Cape Town. She called at Madeira on the way and the soldiers were allowed to go ashore. Unfortunately they imbibed too well, sampling the local beer and Madeira wine. It all concluded with a bruising encounter with the local police in Funchal. The episode was later called *"The Battle of the Golden Gate."*

The *Llanstephan Castle* was retained on the mail service until 1920 and during that period she carried back to Cape Town, the Prime Minister of South Africa, General Louis Botha, following the signing of the Treaty of Versailles.

In the same year the ship was once more in the news. She brought back to England the *Saxon's* passengers when she lost her rudder in a collision with a barge in Cape Town.

Two of the older liners that had been brought out of reserve during the war were refurbished and put back on the mail run for a time. These were the *Norman* and the *Carisbrook Castle*, both of which ended their days on the East Africa run.

The service to East Africa was also disrupted and for an even longer time than the mail service. A limited schedule was started in 1919 but it was another three years before all the ships were back in service. In the period 1919 to 1920 the Company took over a number of 'standard ships' that had been built by the government. At the time Union-Castle were still part of the Royal Mail group and a number of these vessels were allocated to them. The first three were the *Ripley Castle*, *Rosyth Castle* and the *Banbury Castle*. Two further sister ships, similar to the *Banbury Castle*, were added and they were the *Bampton Castle* and *Bratton Castle*. These were all over 4,100 gross tons. Finally the *Dromore Castle* and the *Dundrum Castle* appeared at the end of 1919 and they were slightly larger at 5,200 tons. By 1921 the first of two cargo boats built for Union-Castle came into service, the *Sandgate Castle* of 7,600 gross tons and a year later her sister ship the *Sandown Castle*. Both were used on the South Africa to U.S.A. service.

As a result of the Peace treaty, Germany had to give up her colonies in Africa. The most important of these was German South West Africa, which was placed under the jurisdiction of South Africa and Tanganyika, formerly German East Africa, which became a British Mandated Territory. This brought the ports of Tanga and Dar-es-Salaam into the British sphere, which was of particular interest to the Union-Castle Company. It almost certainly influenced the Directors in their development of the East Coast service. They were perhaps far seeing as they had already opened an office in Mombasa in 1917. Later, in 1920 the territory of British East Africa became the Crown Colony of Kenya.

The intermediate run to Mombasa had recommenced in 1919 with a rather sketchy and limited service. The *Gloucester Castle* and the *Guildford Castle* were used at first and then other ships were added as they were restored and brought back onto the run. It was 1922 before all the ships became available. It was then decided that instead of sending all the liners out via Suez and turning them round at Durban, that each ship would circum-navigate Africa. Two ships sailed out via the Cape, returning to London via the Suez Canal, while two others sailed the opposite way round. The ships used to start the 'Round Africa Service' were the *Llanstephan Castle*, *Guildford Castle*, *Gloucester Castle* and the *Norman*, and later the *Carisbrook Castle*. Shortly afterwards it was decided there should be three sailings in each direction to give an approximately monthly service. It was now possible to go round Africa on the one ship calling at more than twenty ports in some twelve countries. Two new ships were built for this run. The first to appear was the *Llandovery Castle,* 11,640 tons, which made her maiden voyage in 1925 and her sister ship the *Llandaff Castle* which appeared in the following year. She was the last coal burning passenger liner to be built for Union-Castle. She was converted to burn oil shortly before war broke out in 1939. She replaced the *Gloucester Castle,* which returned to the intermediate service.

S.S. Llandovery Castle 1925 - 1953. 10,640 gross tons. Placed on the Round Africa service. Struck a mine off the Spanish coast in 1937 during the Civil War.

By 1926 the deep-water quay at Kilindini had helped considerably with the growing trade that was passing through Mombasa. The first Union-Castle ship to go alongside was the *Crawford Castle.* Another major change on the intermediate liners had come in 1923 when the Second Class had disappeared altogether. Third Class was also done away with in 1934, being redesignated Tourist Class.

The *Cawdor Castle,* which had been added to the fleet as an extra steamer in 1902, ran regularly on the West coast and Mauritius route until the war. Then she was taken over for trooping but she also carried wheat and horses from Canada to Europe. In December 1915 whilst in the Mediterranean, a German submarine that had surfaced attacked her, but she managed to escape. When the war ended she carried back to Cape Town the first contingent of South African troops. After the war she was back on the West coast run until 1923, but was then laid up for a year. She was brought back again on the same run but on the 30th July 1926 she went ashore at Conception Bay, which is South of Walvis

Bay in South West Africa. The crew were all rescued but the *Cawdor Castle* broke up and was lost. The following year the *Chepstow Castle*, which had been acquired in 1915, became the first vessel to berth alongside at the new port of Walvis Bay.

Another near disaster occurred on the 25th March 1926 when the *Garth Castle* ran aground at Ascension Island and flooded one of her holds. The *Kenilworth Castle* was diverted to Ascension, arriving on the 30th March and embarked all the passengers. The *Garth Castle* made her own way to Cape Town where she was repaired.

Life on board the liners at the time of the 'Great Depression' that began in 1926 was not easy. Crew members often had to grease a few palms to get a job on board. Having got a job no one dared to get out of line and lose it. The reminiscences from a deck boy at this time on board a Union-Castle liner gives an idea of the poor conditions that existed:- '*A deck boy was poorly paid and apart from a £1 advance when he signed on, received no further cash until he was paid off at the end of the voyage. There was no such thing at this time as leave pay. A deck boy could be called on to do almost anything on board. Sometimes in the tropics when the trimmers in the engine room collapsed with the heat, the boys had to go down into the stokehold and do a turn at running the coal to the firemen.*

There could be as many as fourteen deck boys on board, some of whom would only be fourteen years old. They lived in very cramped conditions and the bunks consisted of a straw sack and two grey blankets. The pillow they had to provide for themselves. The only treat the boys got was a bottle of pop every Saturday night and two apples on a Thursday. At this time there was no such thing as overtime and refusing to obey an order was considered to be mutiny. The boys ran about the ships decks barefoot. When spreading caustic soda and sand to holystone the decks their feet would be red raw. They could be called on to do all sorts of jobs. They could heave the lead, do a turn on the wheel etc. They had to be able to semaphore, understand the Morse code in case they had to do a wireless watch (only on a cargo ship), and had to learn knots and splices. They also had to know how to sail a lifeboat plus knowing the drill to lower the boats. The deck boys also had to clean the cabins of the Bosun etc. In one case a particular Bosun's Mate was a cruel man and would clout the youngsters quite often. One of the boy's duties was to get coffee beans and grind them in the galley for the Bosun's Mate. On more than one occasion, when the tears were running down his face, he would fling a handful of coffee beans into the grinder followed by a handful of cockroaches. He then ground the lot up together and made the coffee. He would watch him drink it with great satisfaction. Revenge is sweet.'

Another of the intermediate vessels that had a long and varied career was the *Glengorm Castle*, which had been originally called the *German* before her

ROYAL MAIL and FASTEST ROUTE from ENGLAND
to South Africa by Steamers of the
UNION-CASTLE LINE.

Company advertising card showing the Railway bridge over the Zambesi river at the Victoria Falls. Circa 1930.

name was changed soon after the war began. She was first of all converted as a hospital ship and then as an ambulance transport, serving in the Mediterranean. She remained on government service after the war but made one commercial voyage to the Cape in 1921. Following this she was taken over again and fitted out as a troopship and made a number of voyages to India and the Far East. She was handed back to Union-Castle in 1925 and returned to the intermediate service. Her final voyage was a cruise to Mauritius with a full complement of passengers. She stayed in Port Louis for a week before returning to Durban. She then went back to London and in 1930 she was scrapped.

The Union-Castle Line was beginning to build motor ships, and in all, over the next twenty years, the Company built twenty-four of these vessels. The first two ships to appear on the Round Africa service were the *Llangibby Castle* in 1929 with the *Dunbar Castle* following a year later. At the same time the *Durham Castle* and the *Dunluce Castle* were also placed on the same run. The new ships had two rather squat funnels that did nothing to enhance their appearance, as they seemed to be positioned too far forward. Although very similar in appearance they were not sister ships as the *Llangibby Castle* was considerably the larger at just over 12,000 tons. The *Dunbar Castle* was different in one aspect compared with previous intermediates. She had a form of enclosed deck lounge forward instead of the more usual veranda café. She was much the smaller of the two at 10,002 gross tons. In 1934 the *Llangibby Castle* became the first liner where the Company introduced the Round Africa voyages with special fares and advertising in both the United Kingdom and the U.S.A. At around the same time the Company purchased the *Eider* that was to be used as a feeder ship in partnership with the *Hansa* sailing from Southampton to the continental ports. In 1936 the new *Walmer Castle* replaced both these ships.

M.V. Llangibby Castle 1929 - 1954. 11,951 gross tons. Joined the Round Africa service.

In 1926 the *Kildonan Castle* was withdrawn from the mail service and laid up in reserve as the new *Carnarvon Castle* had replaced her. In 1927 she was taken over by the government as a troopship in company with a number of other liners, which included her sister ship the *Kinfauns Castle*. A situation had developed in China that was threatening the so-called Treaty ports of Shanghai, Canton and Jiujiang. This was at a time when the Nationalists under General Chiang Kai-shek were attempting to halt the advance of the Communists who were gaining support in China. This was the beginning of a war that was to go on for more than twenty years. What had brought things to a head in January 1927 was when angry Chinese crowds sized the British concessions in Hankou and Jiujiang. In addition, in Nanking, some Nationalist troops had attacked foreign residents and also the British, American and Japanese Consulates. Seven people were killed as a result of these attacks. It was decided by the British government, because of these attacks with British subjects being killed, that they would send out a division of troops to Shanghai, which was by far the largest British concession. The *Kildonan Castle* was quickly converted and sailed from Southampton for Shanghai carrying the Devonshire Regiment that was part of what was called the Shanghai Defence Force. Her sister ship the *Kinfauns Castle* was also requisitioned and sailed for China. The Cunarder *Megantic* was another liner that sailed at about the same time from Liverpool with troops on board bound for Shanghai.

Meanwhile, the incident in Nanking led to British and American gunboats laying down a barrage that killed some fifteen Chinese troops and four civilians. Some time afterwards the British troops arrived and the International settlement in Shanghai was sealed off with barbed wire fences. When General Chiang Kai-shek arrived in the City, he set about allaying the fears of the foreign residents and curbing the mass militant movement. Chiang settled the Western claims and the troops were withdrawn and they returned to Britain. The *Kildonan Castle* began her career as a troopship when she was rapidly converted only days before she was due to sail on her maiden voyage in 1899. Her career on the mail run had ended in 1926 when she was placed in reserve. On her return from Shanghai she was again taken out of reserve in 1929 for a cargo only voyage and again in 1930 when she took an intermediate voyage before being scrapped.

As early as 1922 a proposal had been put forward to build a new basin to the south of the Victoria and Alfred docks at Cape Town. It would provide four new berths and work started in 1926. By 1933 three berths were available for use. In 1937 fresh proposals were put forward for what was to become the Duncan Dock. Work began that year and the dredged sand and mud to create the new basin would be used to reclaim land in front of the city. When war broke out the increased number of berths was welcome although the new dock was only partially complete, but by 1943 it was finished. Also by 1937 the turning basin at East London had been enlarged, because of the bigger mail ships, and in addition improvements at Port Elizabeth had also been completed.

The small coaster *Ipu*, which had been based at Beira, was sold in 1923. She was replaced by the *Incomati*, which Union-Castle had bought from the Portuguese government. She operated a feeder service from Beira to Chinde, Quelimane, Macusa and Marquival. Chinde, at the time was the only port where the basket to lower passengers disembarking into a tender was still used. This ceased once the Nyasaland railway was completed. The *Incomati* was replaced by the *Rovuma* in 1927.

By 1928 the world was in the grip of a severe depression, far worse than any that had gone before. Trade was badly hit and many ships had to be laid up, One result of this depression was the collapse of the Royal Mail Group in 1930, which at the time controlled around 16% of the worlds passenger liner tonnage. The end result was that the Union-Castle Company eventually regained its independence but it took a long time to unravel all the legal and financial knots.

In the same year an experiment was carried out in South Africa to speed up the internal mail service. Only Cape Town and the surrounding area received the overseas mail quickly. The rest of the country could wait, in some cases for several days. An air service was started which was operated by the South African Air Force. The aircraft left Cape Town on the day the mail ship arrived and flew to Durban, dropping off the mail for Port Elizabeth and East London on the way, and then flew on to Johannesburg. This service was discontinued after a few months. It did lead though in 1929 to Union Airways starting the first commercial air service.

Union-Castle poster for holidays to Madeira and the Canary Islands. Circa 1930's.

Sir Vernon Thompson joined the board of the Union-Castle Company in 1932 and within three months he had been appointed Deputy Chairman. At this time, apart from the growth in fruit exports from South Africa, the depression was at its worst. The Company, by reducing fares and arranging tours managed to show profits, leading up to the ordering of two new mail ships in 1934. This was the period when the Company started seriously to promote the Round Africa voyages and added calls at Tangier and Palma, Majorca, to make it more attractive, particularly for short cruises. Sir Vernon was the driving force in this period, responsible for the revival in the Company's fortunes. In recognition of this in April 1939 he became Chairman of the Union-Castle Mail S.S. Company Limited.

The amount of fruit carried on both mail and intermediate liners grew enormously during the period after the First World War. This was why, in 1935 the first of the Company's refrigerated cargo ships, the *Roslin Castle* appeared. By the time the war began in 1939 five more fruit ships, the *Rothesay Castle*, *Roxburgh Castle*, *Rochester Castle*, *Richmond Castle* and *Rowallan Castle* had all joined the fleet.

S.S. Roslin Castle 1935 - 1967. 7,016 gross tons. The first fully refrigerated cargo ship owned by the Company.

It was in the period before the First World War that shipments of deciduous fruit really began to increase, although very little in the way of citrus fruit was exported at the time. The first significant cargo of citrus fruit had been carried on the *Norman II* in 1908. Twenty years later the picture was rather different. The amount of citrus fruit exported was catching up. The significant factor was the different seasons for the various fruits. Deciduous fruits were shipped from South Africa from December to June. Citrus fruits were shipped from May to

October. This meant that the refrigerated cargo vessels could be utilised for most of the year, with time for the ships to be dry docked and other essential maintenance to be carried out before the new season began. By 1938 exports of fruit to Britain were substantial. Over 4,100,000 packages of deciduous fruit were shipped of which grapes, plums, and peaches were the most important. The shipments of citrus fruits were much the same in quantity with oranges predominating. As time went on different fruits were being despatched e.g. pineapples, melons, avocado's and not forgetting the dried fruits, raisins, sultanas, currants, apricots and peaches.

Apart from fruit, the other exports from South Africa had also grown significantly over the years. In the early days this was a problem for the Line in that there was little cargo for the ships to bring back from South and East Africa. By the mid 1930s both the range and volume of exports had risen, of which the most important from South Africa were:- gold, diamonds, asbestos, copper, chrome, tin, wool, hides & skins, maize, sugar, tobacco and canned crayfish. The same picture can be seen in the variety of exports from East Africa: - sisal, hides, ground nuts, copra, coffee, tea, cotton, soda carbonate, wattle bark, chillies, cloves, tin, copper and tobacco.

The *Dunluce Castle* had been built in 1904 by Harland & Wolff's at Belfast. The other two of this class were built at other yards. She was one of the most popular ships employed on the South and East Africa service. Even when she was getting old a lot of people preferred to travel on her rather than one of the mail ships. In the First World War she was converted to a hospital ship in 1915. Her first voyage was to India and then she was employed in the Mediterranean during the Gallipoli campaign. Later in 1916 she was lent to the Italian Government and sailed up the Adriatic to Balona where she embarked hundreds of Serbs and carried them to Bizerte in North Africa. From the end of 1916 she was for quite some time on the cross Channel run. Following this, she was sent out to East Africa and carried malaria cases from Dar es Salaam to Durban. In 1917 she returned to the Mediterranean theatre and finally she was placed on the Australia run where she was employed until the end of the war. In 1920 she returned to the Mombasa service and in 1931 she was placed on the Round Africa run. In June 1939 she was rescued from being scrapped and became an accommodation ship at Immingham on the outbreak of the war. Later she was moved to Scapa Flow as a depot ship. She had a long career with Union-Castle of some thirty-five years plus five years when she was requisitioned. In 1945 she was scrapped.

By the middle of the 1930's the intermediate vessels, carrying First Class and Tourist class passengers, were despatched from London fortnightly on alternate Fridays for Cape Town, Port Elizabeth, East London, Natal , Lourenco Marques and also frequently to Beira. These liners called alternately at Las Palmas, Gran Canaria and Santa Cruz, Teneriffe. They also called once a month with the mails at Ascension and St.Helena, under contract to His Majesty's Government. In addition a vessel was despatched at intervals, via the Canary Islands and South Africa to Mauritius. Vessels also called every four weeks at Lobito Bay in Angola and Walvis Bay outward bound and as required on the homeward voyage.

The *Llandaff Castle* was another popular ship on the Round Africa run. On one voyage in the 1930's, when as she was approaching Zanzibar she ran aground on one of the numerous sandbanks. Efforts were made by going astern using the ship's engines to get her afloat again, but without success. In the end dhows and other small craft were called in. They tied up to the stern of the ship and then ran out their anchors and managed to heave her off.

By now each month on a Thursday a passenger ship was despatched from London calling at Tangier, Gibraltar, Palma (Majorca), Marseilles, Genoa, Port Said, Suez, Port Sudan, Aden to Mombasa thence to Tanga, Zanzibar, Dar-es-Salaam., Port Amelia, Mozambique, Beira, Lourenco Marques, the South African ports, St. Helena, Ascension and the Canary Islands. In addition a further vessel also sailed monthly from London via the West coast calling at the same ports, returning through the Suez Canal. The original itinerary had been changed earlier when the port of Genoa replaced Naples.

It was some time before the intermediate ships were built with swimming pools. Only towards the end of the 1930's when new ships were built did they include a pool. Prior to that, when the weather became warm a wooden framed swimming pool would be rigged on the open deck. This was greatly appreciated by the passengers, particularly in the steamy heat of the East Coast. These pools were around twenty feet long by fifteen wide and six feet deep. Diving was not allowed. It was even longer before air conditioning appeared and it could be stifling in the cabins despite the punkah louvre. They moved the air around but made little difference. The heat was at its worst whilst the ship was in port. At least at sea, provided you had a cabin with a porthole, and were lucky enough to have a wind scoop, which fitted, into that porthole, and then this would help to keep the cabin very much cooler than would otherwise have been the case.

In the spring and summer months continental cruises continued in connection with the Company's intermediate ships from London to Antwerp, Rotterdam, Hamburg and return to load and discharge cargo. These trips were of ten or eleven days duration and the fare (First Class only) was described as extremely moderate.

Cruises to Mauritius from South Africa were also arranged around December and January, extending into February when it was possible to spend between two and four weeks on board, according to the port of embarkation. The ships departed from Cape Town and called, sometimes at Mossel Bay, Port Elizabeth, East London, Durban, Lourenco Marques and thence to Mauritius.

They returned to Cape Town via Durban, East London and Port Elizabeth. These were very popular cruises, as of course they were operated at the peak holiday time in South Africa. The length of the cruises depended on the port of departure and return.

Towards the end of the 1930's cruising in general became very popular with ships providing numerous diversions and amusements when on the high seas, and a variety of ports of call for passengers to explore. They were not necessarily special voyages for cruising passengers only, but regular commercial ventures. For example, Union-Castle advertised special holiday tours of about ten weeks around Africa for the modest sums of £100 (First Class) and £50 (Tourist class), The *Llandovery Castle* was due to sail from London on the 28th December 1935 via the East coast and the *Durham Castle* followed a week later on the 3rd January 1936 via the West coast. The publicity at the time stated that:- *"It would be difficult to find a similar journey which provided so wide a variety of scenery and interests and entailed so little exertion."* Some twelve months later the *Llandovery Castle* set off again on a Round Africa voyage. She had entered the Mediterranean and following her call at Palma was on her way to Marseilles. The Spanish Civil War had begun and the *Llandovery Castle* was unfortunate enough to hit a mine off the Spanish coast. She was able to limp into the small harbour of Port Vendres where it took nearly three months to carry out temporary repairs to her forward holds before she could steam to Genoa, where major repairs were carried out.

During this period of time much had changed on the East African coast but the Arab dhows were still operating in large numbers. In 1934, 3,525 dhows entered the harbour at Zanzibar. Many of these of course would have been the smaller coastal dhows, which would have called at Zanzibar a number of times during the course of the year.

In addition to the publicity for the Round Africa ships winter sailings, the mail boats were advertised as well, for those wishing to escape the cold weather in Britain by travelling to South Africa. In line with this, the Mount Nelson Hotel in Cape Town was advertising inclusive terms from 21/- per day with accommodation for 175 visitors; Accommodation included private self-contained suites, and double and single bedrooms with private bathrooms.

Other Shipping Companies were also advertising cruises at the same time. For example the Cunard-White Star Company's *Franconia* was going on a world cruise of more than five months, with fares ranging from £395, which included the cost of the shore excursions. The *Strathmore* of the P. & O. Company was making a short cruise to the Mediterranean and then a four-week cruise to the West Indies. Lamport & Holt Line, Royal Mail and the Bibby Line were amongst other companies advertising a range of cruises at very competitive prices.

As the Round Africa cruises became more popular, so the number and

93

length of excursions at the various ports increased. By 1938 the shore excursion booklet issued by Union-Castle for passengers contained forty-six pages and covered twenty-four ports. The range of different tours was extensive as were the methods of transport. In Tangier for example the sightseeing tour was by donkey. In Port Said if you went to Cairo to see the Pyramids you could travel by car, coach, train and camel. At Port Sudan you could go on the glass bottomed boat to view the coral gardens. A flight in a two or four seater plane was possible at Beira to view the game, plus a boat trip up the Buzi River to see the hundreds of crocodiles and hippopotamus. The number of tours that were possible could be a little bewildering at first. Who would think that you could go on seven different excursions on the small island of Zanzibar? The Company were careful to point out that these excursions were run by agents at the various ports. In many cases they were organised by Thomas Cook & Son/Wagon-Lits Limited

The next two ships ordered for the Round Africa run were the *Dunnottar Castle* and the *Dunvegan Castle*, both of which were around 15,000 gross tons, considerably larger than any of their predecessors. They were also much faster and were used initially between 1936 and 1938 on the mail run. This was while the older mail ships went back to Harland and Wolff's shipyards to be altered so that they could reach the speed required for the new mail contract. Union-Castle Line attracted quite a lot of attention in the middle thirties when in 1936 they brought four new liners into service. The *Stirling Castle* and the *Athlone Castle* joined the mail ship fleet plus the *Dunnottar Castle* and *Dunvegan Castle*, destined for the Round Africa service eventually.

M.V. Dunnottar Castle 1936 - 1958. 15,002 gross tons. Intended for the Round Africa route. Filled in initially on the mail run.

94

The introduction of these two new intermediate vessels meant a considerable change when compared with the earlier ships and much comment was made about their modern design and distinctive appearance. The First Class provided accommodation for 258 passengers in two or three berth rooms whilst the Tourist Class could accommodate 250 in two or four berth cabins. The First Class lounge on the upper promenade deck had windows on three sides and was decorated with a pleasant combination of honey-coloured veneers and painted wall surfaces. The Tourist Class public rooms were said to be designed for comfort and appearance and included a dining saloon large enough to accommodate all the passengers at one sitting. When the *Dunnottar Castle* joined the Round Africa service she inaugurated an additional homeward bound call at Walvis Bay.

Two further ships were soon ordered for the Round Africa service. These were to have South African names, *Durban Castle* and *Pretoria Castle*. They were both a slightly larger version of the successful *Dunnottar Castle* type. By April 1939 all the new liners were in service. Since 1930 the Company had built five mail ships and five intermediate vessels, not to mention six refrigerated cargo vessels and a small feeder ship, the *Walmer Castle*. The Company now had probably the most modern fleet in the world and also the best looking.

M.V. Pretoria Castle. 1938 - 1962. 17,383 gross tons. Delivered for the Round Africa service. After two voyages was requisitioned as an Armed Merchant Cruiser.

In the twenty years since the war had ended, Union-Castle had only one casualty amongst the passenger liners, This was the *Guildford Castle*, an intermediate which was rammed and sunk on the 1st June 1933 by the Blue

Funnel liner *Stentor* in the river Elbe. The German pilot was held responsible for the collision. The *Grantully Castle* was brought out of reserve to replace the *Guildford Castle*.

In addition to the building programme and the alterations to the older mail ships, in 1939 three of the older intermediate ships, the *Llanstephan Castle*, *Llandovery Castle* and *Llandaff Castle* had been converted from coal burning to oil burning. This left only the *Gloucester Castle* as a coal burner but she was in reserve and was expected to be scrapped in the near future.

In June 1937 the cargo ship *Sandgate Castle*, having left New York on her way to Cape Town, caught fire some 350 miles from Bermuda. The crew abandoned ship and were picked up by the *President Pierce* three days later. The *Sandgate Castle* was sighted by the Italian liner *Conte de Savoia* on the 30th June when she was still burning. She sank shortly afterwards.

CHAPTER 6 - WORLD WAR TWO

When war broke out on the 3rd September 1939 the Union-Castle Line had a fleet of liners, eight of which were mail ships and ten intermediates. In addition there were ten general and refrigerated cargo vessels, plus one small coaster the *Rovuma*, based at Beira and one feeder ship based at Southampton. A total of thirty ships with a combined gross tonnage of 383,000 tons.

The *Edinburgh Castle* had been laid up in 1939 but when the war began the Admiralty bought her. She was sent to Freetown as the base ship for the Convoy Escort Force. She spent the entire war there as an accommodation ship. When the war was over she was towed out to sea and sunk. The Navy at the time would have liked the *Edinburgh Castle's* sister ship, the *Balmoral Castle*. Unfortunately she had just gone for scrap and was being broken up.

Three of the intermediates were selected to be converted to armed merchant cruisers. These were the *Dunvegan Castle*, *Dunnottar Castle* and the newest ship the *Pretoria Castle*. The *Carnarvon Castle* was the only mail ship to become an armed merchant cruiser, and she later became a troop transport. The *Dunnottar Castle's* sailing from London was cancelled several days before the war began and she was sent to Belfast for conversion. She was commissioned on the 14th October and her main armament was seven six-inch guns and two three-inch anti-aircraft guns. Because of the numbers of people who had booked to return to East Africa, the *Gloucester Castle* was brought out of reserve to take the *Dunnottar Castle's* place.

R.M.M.V. Carnarvon Castle. 1926 - 1963. 20,122 gross tons. Requisitioned as an Armed Merchant Cruiser, operating mainly in the South Atlantic.

The *Dunvegan Castle* was due to leave East London at 2.p.m. on the day that war was declared. She was about to sail on her normal voyage up the East Coast. The pilot was already on board when a cable was received from the Admiralty instructing her to return immediately to the United Kingdom. All the passengers had to disembark and their baggage was also unloaded and she sailed the same night for Cape Town. When she arrived all her cargo for East African ports was discharged and cargo for England loaded. She was then painted grey overall and sailed for London via Freetown. She was soon followed by the *Pretoria Castle* as she also had instructions to return straight away to the United Kingdom. The three intermediate liners, together with the *Carnarvon Castle* were mainly employed on convoy duty between Freetown and the Cape.

The *Durban Castle* was also taken over in September 1939 and initially she was converted to a troopship. Later she carried the King and Queen of Greece and their family on a voyage from Durban back to England. They had fled to Egypt when the German army invaded Greece.

Within a short period of time all the other mail ships became troop transports, visiting a multiplicity of nations. The *Capetown Castle* for example was the only Union-Castle liner to ever pass through the Straits of Magellan. She sailed from Cape Town through the Straits and up the West coast of South America. She then passed through the Panama Canal and continued up the East coast of America to New York. The *Stirling Castle* was used mainly to carry American troops to Britain. On one voyage she carried 6,000 men, a record for the Company. She held a second record when she carried the England cricket team to Australia in 1947 and then later she carried the England team again to South Africa. The *Athlone Castle* was also a troopship on the North American route. Both returned to the mail route in 1947.

The German ship *Watussi* of the Woermann Line had left Durban just before war broke out. She headed for Lourenco Marques in Portuguese Territory for shelter where she remained for some time. As she resembled the older two funnel liners on the mail run, the Germans painted her in Union-Castle colours and set off to steam round the Cape and back to Germany. She was soon spotted by a South African Air Force plane about one hundred miles south of Cape Point and was ordered to alter course and head for Simonstown. The disguise might have worked but unfortunately for the enemy, the Company was no longer using these two funnel liners. The last one, the *Edinburgh Castle* had already been taken over by the British Navy. A cruiser was sent to intercept the *Watussi* but by the time she arrived on the scene the ship was on fire and sinking. The passengers and crew on board were all rescued and spent the war in internment in South Africa.

One of the intermediate liners, the *Dunbar Castle* was an early wartime casualty. On the 9th June 1940 she had sailed from London on her way to join up with a convoy. She was en route to Beira when she struck a mine and sank in the English Channel off Ramsgate. A motor barge picked up one hundred survivors but nine lives were lost including the Captain. The vessel broke in two by the bridge and sank in twenty minutes. She went down in shallow water and her two funnels were visible until 1949. Then demolition charges were laid and she was blown up.

R.M.S. Capetown Castle 1938 - 1967. 27,000 gross tons. Early 1940 Passenger List before the ship was requisitioned for trooping. No departure port or date of sailing is given.

R.M.M.V. Athlone Castle 1936 - 1965. 25,564 gross tons. She was requisitioned as a troopship and operated mainly between the U.S.A. and Britain.

Another early casualty, although not from enemy action was the *Rothesay Castle*. She was one of the refrigerated cargo ships and was on her way from New York to Glasgow. She ran ashore on the Isle of Islay. In addition, the *Dunvegan Castle's* career as an armed merchant cruiser was all too brief. She was torpedoed in the North Atlantic off the West Coast of Eire in August 1940. She was one of the escort ships accompanying a convoy on its way to Freetown. She remained afloat for some time but sank the following day. There were 277 crew members on board of whom 250 were saved.

Some rapid changes took place in the early days of the war. Both the Port of London and Southampton became closed to normal liner traffic and all these ships began to operate from either Liverpool or Glasgow. This meant that many of the shore staff of the shipping companies had to move to these ports. As soon as the war started Sir Vernon Thompson was made Director of Commercial Services at the Board of Trade. By November 1939 a separate Ministry of Shipping was established and Sir Vernon became the Principal Adviser and Controller of Commercial Shipping. In January of the following year the Government requisitioned all British ships. In May 1941, the Ministry of Shipping merged with the Ministry of War Transport with Sir Vernon continuing his role until early in 1946.

The war got away to a fairly slow start. Very little happened in the first six months and this became known as the 'phoney war'. The British Expeditionary

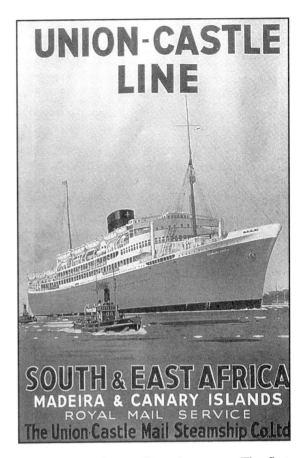

R.M.M.V. Stirling Castle 1936 - 1966. 25,550 gross tons. Also became a troopship on the North American run. Carried over 6,000 troops on one voyage.

Force was shipped to France with little interference from the enemy. The first problem came with the new magnetic mines that were sown by the Germans around the British coast. At first there was no known way of counteracting these mines and they became a real threat, sinking many ships.

Two of the old Union-Castle intermediate liners had been sold for scrap early in 1939. Before they went to the breakers the Admiralty stepped in and commandeered them for use as depot ships. The *Durham Castle* was being towed to Scapa Flow for this purpose when she struck a mine off Cromarty and sank. The *Dunluce Castle* became an accommodation ship.

The 'phoney war' ended abruptly in the spring of 1940 when Germany invaded both Norway and Denmark. Then it was the turn of Belgium, Holland and Luxembourg and soon the Panzers were rolling into France. This brought about the collapse of the French Army in June, which led to the evacuation of the British Expeditionary Force from Dunkirk.

The *Dundrum Castle* was one of the Company's general cargo boats of just over 5,000 gross tons. She sailed from Southampton with a military cargo in May 1940 which was to be off loaded at Dunkirk. When she arrived at the port the evacuation of British troops had already begun and the ship was ordered to return to Southampton with her cargo. Later she sailed, still with the same cargo, to St. Nazaire. She waited for several days but by then the situation had begun to change rapidly.

The beginning of the collapse of French resistance by June 15th meant that the R.A.F. had to fly their remaining aircraft back to England. As most of the planes were single seater fighters, the ground crews were to be evacuated from St. Nazaire. In addition there were many troops and civilians, including women and children heading for the port. By the 16th June there were an estimated 98,000 troops and others, both British and French converging on St. Nazaire and the nearby port of Nantes, further up the Loire. That same day some 13,000 were evacuated, many on the Cunard, White Star liner *Franconia*, which suffered some damage from air attacks. The *Georgic*, also a Cunard liner, was present, and sailed back to England with many troops on board after only suffering minor damage.

The *Lancastria*, also a Cunard liner, had just returned to Britain, from evacuating troops from Norway. As soon as the soldiers disembarked she was sent post haste to St. Nazaire. The Captain had wanted to discharge the bulk of his fuel oil before sailing, but the authorities did not allow him to. There was no time to lose. The *Lancastria* arrived at St.Nazaire. at 6 a.m. on the 17th June and she anchored off in the Bay. The Captain was instructed to disregard International Law regarding the number of passengers that could be carried. The Orient Line passenger vessel *Oronsay*, also arrived to take part in the evacuation. Soon destroyers including H.M.S. *Highlander* and other smaller craft were ferrying troops out to the two 17,000 ton liners. There were also some ten other smaller ships waiting to take part in the evacuation, including the *Dundrum Castle*. By this time evacuation from the Channel ports and St. Malo and Brest had ceased. Time was rapidly running out.

Around mid day German aircraft arrived overhead bombing the port of St. Nazaire and the merchantmen, including the *Dundrum Castle*, which was alongside. Those ships that were able put up a barrage with their A.A. guns. Later the *Dundrum Castle* got her orders to sail. She was late leaving because at the last moment she took on board more than five hundred troops and civilians. She passed through the lock after 2 p.m. and steamed down the river Loire making good her escape into the Bay. She was still carrying her military cargo. Troops were still being ferried out to the two big ships, which were protected by Naval ships and anti-submarine vessels. The *Lancastria* had taken on board many troops; far beyond the number she should have carried. The Chief Purser admitted that after 6,000 had come on board, he stopped counting. Some estimates put the total on board including crew at 9,000.

All the ships were told to wait so that they could sail in convoy. It was thought that German submarines were in the area. Some fighter cover from

England was given but they could not stay over the ships for long. The fighter planes had not got a long enough range for more than a short stay. In addition, a decision had been taken to conserve the fighter aircraft and the pilots for the expected battle to come. In the early afternoon the *Oronsay* was hit and the bridge was damaged. She was taking in water and the pumps were losing the battle to keep her afloat. The Captain, who had been injured, gave the orders to sail and she arrived back in England safely.

Shortly before 4 p.m., out of a clear blue sky came seventeen Dornier bombers from the Luftwaffe Umbrella Geschwader which attacked the ships from out of the sun. The *Lancastria* was a prime target and she was soon hit. The first bomb struck the number two hold that contained eight hundred R.A.F. personnel. A second went down the funnel and a third sliced open the side of the ship. A fourth bomb released the 1,400 tons of fuel oil into the sea. The decision to sail before off loading the bulk of the oil was now going to contribute to the disaster. Attempts were made to lower the lifeboats but because the ship was listing many could not be successfully launched. In addition, because of the fuel oil on the water, the efforts of survivors to swim to safety were hampered. Before long the ship had turned onto her port side trapping thousands inside the hull. As the ship's propellers appeared out of the water, men were standing on the side of the ship. The *Lancastria* was a blazing inferno when she sank in less than twenty-five minutes. By this time some of the oil on the surface of the water was burning.

In company with other ships, including the *Glenaffaric, Fabian* and *John Holt*, the *Dundrum Castle* launched two of her lifeboats, one in the charge of Mr.D.Klasen, chief officer and the other in the charge of Mr.W.Shannon, second officer. The work of rescue was slow and painful because of the thick fuel oil. *H.M.S.Havelock* and the anti-submarine vessel *Cambridgeshire* were quickly on the scene picking up survivors. In addition small French boats put out to sea from the port to assist while the air attacks continued. By this time the German aircraft that were still overhead were machine-gunning the survivors in the water.

The *Dundrum Castle's* lifeboats were amongst the last to leave the scene with the crews absolutely exhausted. They returned to the ship with more than 120 survivors. She now had on board around six hundred and fifty people, virtually standing shoulder to shoulder. They had very little food on board as there had been no opportunity to take on any stores.. However, they managed to rustle up hot soup for everyone. At 11p.m. the *Dundrum Castle* was instructed to join the next convoy and she sailed for Southampton where she landed the troops and civilians. The *Dundrum Castle* was very lucky as she only suffered minor damage.

Only 2,447 survivors were rescued and it is estimated that it is possible that as many as 6,000 or more died. At the time, the loss of life was so great that

Winston Churchill ordered a news blackout because of the effect this disaster would have on morale. He described it as 'the most terrible disaster in British Naval history.' Certainly, it was Britain's worst maritime disaster ever. The 'D' notice on the sinking of the *Lancastria* was lifted after the New York Times had broken the news of the sinking nine days later, on the 26th June, 1940. They also included some of the dramatic photographs. Not many photographs have survived, as Naval personnel were not allowed cameras on the ships. One crewmember on board *H.M.S. Highlander* disobeyed the orders and took some remarkable photographs that were later published. Once the 'D' notice was lifted, the British newspapers were able to publish the news. *The Times* article was as follows:

THE LANCASTRIA SUNK.

"As reported in our later editions yesterday. The loss of the Cunard White Star liner Lancastria off the French port of St. Nazaire, as she was evacuating members of the B.E.F. (British Expeditionary Force) on the day that the Petain government capitulated, has now been revealed. Nobody knows exactly how many were on board, but the number was probably about 5,000 of whom about 2,500 were saved. Most of the casualties were British soldiers but there were also on board 600 R.A.F. officers and men and a few British civilians who had held official positions in France. Nearly all of them had come from Nantes, which had been used as an assembling ground for British troops of all units. St.Nazaire was one of the last ports available for the evacuation of British troops and many thousands embarked there. A number of air raids had already been carried out on St. Nazaire but the damage done had been slight and the casualties surprisingly few. The embarkation had not been completed when the shipping was attacked by a strong formation of Junkers 87 Dive-bombers. Three bombs hit the Lancastria."

Sixty years on, what exactly happened on that terrible day is not totally clear. This is not altogether surprising because of the chaotic conditions and the pressure that existed to bring home as many military personnel as possible. How many troops were taken prisoners of war and how many actually reached England is not easy to determine now. There are rumours of government documents relating to the disaster remaining as still an official secret. No evidence of this can be found in the Public Record Office, which holds the National Archives. The questions that are asked include –Who gave the orders to the Captain to ignore International Law on the number of passengers that could be carried? Also who gave the order for the ship to sail without off loading most of her fuel oil? In addition, apart from insufficient boats there were only about 2,000 lifejackets on board. To compound the disaster, there had been no time for a boat drill or even to instruct the soldiers in what to do if they had to jump over the side. Many died with lifejackets on when their necks were broken when they hit the water.

In June 2000, survivors of the fourth worst shipping disaster world wide, made a pilgrimage to the spot where the *Lancastria* sank. Survivors laid wreaths, watched by thousands of local residents and veterans on shore. The position where the ship sank is a French designated war grave and remains untouched. Visits by the survivors were also made to the cemeteries where troops who lost their lives were buried. The Royal British Legion organised the pilgrimage in conjunction with the Lancastria Association

The two Armed Merchant cruisers *Carnarvon Castle* and *Pretoria Castle* both operated mainly in the South Atlantic and were involved in the search for the German pocket battleship *Admiral Scheer*. However, she slipped through the net and sank a number of merchant ships before returning to Germany. It was in December 1940 when the *Carnarvon Castle* met up with the German raider *Thor*. She did not respond to signals when she was sighted and the *Carnarvon Castle* fired a warning shot. The response from the *Thor* was to hoist her battle ensign and fire several salvos in reply.

The German ship was better armed and it was some time before the *Carnarvon Castle* was in range. By then though she had been hit and her electrical control systems were out of action. She did record hits on the *Thor* who responded by firing two torpedoes. The *Carnarvon Castle* altered course and both torpedoes missed. Without proper fire control the British ship was in difficulties although one shot was seen to hit just below the *Thor's* bridge. The enemy laid down a smoke screen and with night falling she escaped. The *Carnarvon* Castle was ordered into Montevideo where temporary repairs were carried out before she sailed for Cape Town.

Earlier in 1940 the *Llangibby Castle* was still on her normal Round Africa schedule. She left London in April and called at Genoa as usual. The Italians were extremely hostile and none of the passengers were allowed to go ashore. Within a matter of weeks Italy had entered the war on the side of Germany. This meant that it was now too dangerous for shipping to sail through the Mediterranean. The route around the Cape became the only way to reach the Far and Middle East. Towards the end of that year the Axis powers attention was drawn towards Egypt as a way to India and beyond. The Italian forces in Libya launched an attack and began to advance on Cairo. It was then that a campaign was begun by Britain against the Italian Colonies in the Horn of Africa. Two of the Union-Castle intermediate ships, the *Llandaff Castle* and the *Llangibby* Castle were used to transport troops, guns and military equipment from South Africa to this new theatre of war. The *Llandaff Castle* was in the convoy that was attacked by the German heavy cruiser, *Admiral Hipper*, but she escaped unscathed. The cruiser H.M.S *Berwick* was able to force the *Hipper* to break off the action. Following this, The *Llandaff Castle* spent most of her time as a troopship plying between Durban and Suez, but she did not survive the war.

Only one of the Company's intermediate vessels was taken over as a hospital ship this time, unlike the First World War. The *Llandovery Castle* was converted at Southampton in November 1940. The city was heavily bombed in the Blitz and during one of the air raids the *Llandovery Castle* was badly damaged. She was hit again at Suez in 1941 where she escaped with only minor damage. In the following year she carried over 900 wounded Italian prisoners to Smyrna where they were exchanged for British wounded soldiers. Later, in the Mediterranean, she came under attack from the air several times both in Tobruk and at sea, on her way to Alexandria. She was the last hospital ship to leave Tobruk before the town was over-run. In July 1943 she was the hospital ship assigned to Operation 'Husky', which was the code word for the invasion of Sicily. She was a ship that appeared to have a charmed life and she survived to rejoin the Round Africa service. During the war she steamed over 250,000 miles and carried nearly 40,000 wounded.

The *Llanstephan Castle*, which had come through the First World War, arrived in Cape Town in August 1940 carrying three hundred children that had been evacuated from the United Kingdom. Shortly afterwards the British government stopped sending children overseas because of the risks involved. One liner carrying many children had been sunk in the North Atlantic. In June 1941, following the invasion of Russia by Germany, Britain began to send military supplies to Murmansk. The *Llanstephan Castle* was the Commodore ship of the first of the Russian Arctic convoys. She left Liverpool on the 8th August 1941 and arrived in Archangel on September 1st after an uneventful voyage. Later convoys were not to be so fortunate. The aircraft that had been brought from England were assembled in Archangel and then flown to Murmansk. On her return voyage to Britain she carried 200 Polish airmen who had been released by the Russians and they subsequently joined the Royal Air Force. Despite many adventures the *Llanstephan Castle* survived once again to return to peacetime service on the Round Africa run.

The author, Nicholas Montserrat, was a frequent traveller on Union-Castle ships after the war. In 1941 though he was first Lieutenant on the corvette *Campanula* and Charles Cuthbertson, who prior to the war was a deck officer on Union-Castle, was commander of the *Zinnia*. The two men first met after the tragic passage of convoy OG71. After the war when he wrote the book *'The Cruel Sea'* Montserrat based one of the main characters, Lieutenant Commander Ericson, on Cuthbertson. He went on to command a destroyer in 1943, operating in the North Atlantic. Later he commanded a frigate and became Senior Officer of an escort flotilla. He returned to Union-Castle in

1946 and in 1948 was Master of the *Sandown Castle*.

The feeder ship, *Walmer Castle*, which was based at Southampton, was requisitioned firstly as a supply ship and was based at Scapa Flow. In 1941 she was converted to a rescue ship. These were small ships that were attached to convoys to pick up survivors when ships were sunk. Unfortunately her career was brief as within little more than a month she was sunk. She was attached to a convoy heading for Gibraltar that came under heavy attack from the air. The *Walmer* had rescued fifty-eight survivors from two ships that had been torpedoed. By the time she got under way again the convoy had disappeared over the horizon. When dawn broke she was still a long way behind. Later on in the morning she was attacked from the air but by skilful steering the ship managed to avoid the first bombs. Their luck did not last though for the ship was severely damaged and caught fire. The *Walmer Castle* had to be abandoned but most of the boats were destroyed or damaged. Most of the crew and survivors got away on life rafts but thirteen of the crew stayed on board. In the afternoon two Naval ships arrived on the scene and rescued the survivors. The *Walmer Castle* was then sunk by gunfire. Eleven members of the crew including the Captain were killed plus two crew members who were survivors from the ships that had been sunk beforehand.

In the summer of 1941 the *Pretoria Castle* was one of two merchant cruisers fitted out at Newport News, Virginia, U.S.A. to carry two Fairey Seafox seaplanes. In addition she was supplied with a catapult and a crane for recovery. The equipment was rather old, as it had been removed from the battleship H.M.S. *Warspite*. The *Pretoria Castle* carried two pilots, two observers and a maintenance crew of eight. One of the planes was kept permanently on the catapult while the other was housed in a sunken hangar, which had been the ship's swimming pool. The demise of the pool did not go down well with the crew who did briefly contemplate mutiny. She continued to operate in the South Atlantic on convoy duty and the Seafox's were used mainly for reconnaissance and they were armed with a single machine gun and carried small bombs. The planes would have to land in the lee of the ship for recovery and the ship's crane was used to hoist them aboard.

The aircraft had a range of about 440 miles and regular search missions were flown both ahead and to port and starboard of the convoy. The most difficult part of these operations was the landing. If the sea was choppy it could be extremely hazardous. On one occasion a Seafox was returning short of fuel and on reaching the point where they expected to sight the *Pretoria Castle* there was no sign of her. The pilot managed to get off a radio message before the engine cut out. As the plane touched down in the heavy swell the sea broke the struts of one of the floats. It was some time before the *Pretoria Castle* arrived on the scene and because of the conditions it took a long time to recover the crew and the plane, which was in a very poor state.

By December 1941 Japan had entered the war and reinforcements were to be sent by Britain and from Australia and elsewhere to Malaya and Singapore. Early in January a convoy sailed from the Clyde and amongst the troopships was the *Llangibby Castle*. Four days later she was hit in the stern by a torpedo. There were 1,500 troops on board of which twenty-six were killed. The rudder of the ship had been virtually destroyed and was useless. An escort could not be spared from the convoy and so she started to make her way to the Azores steering the ship by using her engines. She could only make 9 knots and she was soon under attack from the air. The aircraft dropped its bombs but missed, and the anti-aircraft guns on the ship replied. They scored a hit and the plane broke off the attack and was last seen trailing black smoke and losing height

Fortunately the ship suffered no further attacks and three days later the crippled liner arrived in Horta Bay in the Azores. Portugal was a neutral country in the war and they were allowed to stay for fourteen days. There was not a great deal they could do to repair the damage and the Germans became aware of where she was. By the time she left on the 2nd February a U boat pack was waiting for her. She now had an escort of three destroyers and just as the *Llangibby Castle* left port one of the destroyers rammed and sank a submarine. Until dark a running battle went on between the escorts and the U boats with the naval guns firing star shells to light up the scene and depth charges were being dropped. The *Llangibby Castle* was under tow by a tug to try to get her out of the danger zone as quickly as possible. The following morning she cast off the tow and resumed her zigzag course towards Gibraltar. Several more attacks were made by the U boats without success and by February 6th she was near enough to Gibraltar for air cover to be provided. Two days later she arrived at the Rock and the troops disembarked. For the whole voyage after she was hit, the troops had remained on deck only going below for meals. She remained at Gibraltar for almost two months. Still without a rudder she then sailed for the United Kingdom where she arrived safely six days later.

Before the Second World War had begun the *Gloucester Castle* was on the list to be scrapped. She was twenty-nine years old and because she was waiting to go to the breakers she had not been modernised. She still had coal-fired bunkers and struggled to make 10 knots. The Government did not take her over from Union-Castle when war broke out. She was laid up at the time so she was brought out of retirement to go back on the South African run. Nobody wanted her really, because she was something of a liability. In convoy she churned out so much heavy black smoke it was visible for miles. In addition she could not keep her station in a convoy that was doing 9 knots. In the period immediately before the war she regularly took twenty-three days to reach Cape Town calling at Ascension and St. Helena. In 1942 the Captain was so incensed about the state of the ship that he complained to Sir Vernon Thompson.

Freetown which was the assembly port for North bound vessels had found

108

the *Gloucester Castle's* slow speed a problem and she had to be placed in a convoy that was only making just over 7 knots. She really was the 'Goslowster Castle' as she was nicknamed. The Captain expressed his opinion to Sir Vernon that passengers should not be carried in such a slow old ship. Because of the state of the liner her passenger certificate was cancelled and she was only allowed to carry twelve passengers like any of the company's other cargo vessels.

The *Gloucester Castle* left Liverpool on the 21st June 1942. She was en route to Cape Town without making any stops on the way. A dozen women and children were taking passage on board to join their fathers at the Naval base at Simonstown. She started off in convoy but when it was considered safe she went on her way alone heading for Cape Town. Nothing more was heard of her and eventually two months later the Admiralty notified Union-Castle that the ship had to be presumed lost.

It was not until nearly twelve months later that Captain Griffiths of the *Gemstone*, which had also been sunk, had briefly met up on board the German tanker with the survivors from the *Gloucester Castle*. He wrote to his wife from Germany that he had met a woman, a teenage girl and two boys. He was not permitted by the German censors to give any details, not even the name of the ship. However, about the same time the Admiralty received the names of thirty of the crew that were held at Osaka. Nothing more was learnt of the fate of the ship until the end of the war.

It was on the night of the 15th July that the blacked out *Gloucester Castle* was steaming south towards the Cape when suddenly she was under fire with shells hitting her. The radio operator was killed immediately and the equipment was destroyed. The ship started to list and settle and within minutes she had gone down. They had only managed to launch one boat but the raider also lowered her boats to pick up survivors. Of the 154 people on board only 61 were rescued which included four of the passengers. The German crew were surprised that there were passengers on board as they thought they had sunk a cargo boat. The raider was the *Michel*, a former merchant ship. The survivors were held on board her before they were transferred to the tanker *Charlotte Schliemann*. The conditions on board were dreadful, far worse than on the *Michel*. It was several weeks before the tanker got underway and headed out of the area but her destination was not Germany but Japan. In September she put in to Singapore where some of the men were taken ashore by the Japanese. Included were some of the crew of the *Gloucester Castle*. The ship then sailed for her final destination, Yokohama where she arrived on October19th. The prisoners were handed over to the Japanese. The four passengers were placed in an internment camp at Kobe and the remainder of the crew were sent to Osaka where they worked in the dockyards. It was only when the war in the Far East ended and all prisoners were repatriated that the full story of what had occurred became known. Only 59 of the survivors lived to tell the tale as two crew members had died in captivity.

Also in 1942 the *Llandaff Castle* was taking part in the successful landings on the island of Madagascar. Once this operation was completed she returned to her regular run between Suez and Durban. In November that year she sailed from Suez and after calls at Mombasa and Dar-es-Salaam she sailed for Durban. When she was some 300 miles South East of Lourenco Marques three torpedoes hit her. Lifeboats and rafts were launched and all on board with the exception of two men got away safely before the ship sank. One of the boats had a radio and was able to transmit a message giving their position. Within 36 hours Naval ships arrived and picked up the survivors from two boats. One boat with 47 people on board was missing. It had landed safely on a beach in Zululand. Two Zulus spotted them from the shore and a message for help was sent by runner to the nearest town. Eventually transport arrived and all the survivors were taken to Durban.

It was only some years after the war was over that the Company found out the details about this incident. Not only had the Zulus sent for help but they also looked after the survivors in their village providing them with food etc. Help took some time as the nearest town was some sixty miles away and Zulu runners took the message. The Zulu, Mphaleni Zikali, who was responsible for providing all the help had never been thanked beyond receiving the compass from the boat. When Sir Vernon Thompson heard the story he gave instructions that three cattle should be sent together with other gifts plus an ox to be roasted to provide a feast for the whole village.

The Admiralty bought the *Pretoria Castle* to convert her to become an auxiliary aircraft carrier. She was designed to carry twenty-one aircraft but she was only used for a short while in the Atlantic. She was sent to Iceland carrying American personnel to the island base and flew anti-submarine patrols on the way. Whilst there, some redundant Swordfish aircraft were collected for return to Britain. While one of the Swordfish was waiting to land on PC (as she was affectionately known) the pilot got into a mock dogfight with a US Air Force fighter. Using the Swordfish's old trick which was used to good effect against the German fighters, the pilot dived and then turned sharply so that the American pilot over shot and ended up in the drink.

Soon after her return to England PC became a trials and training carrier. The new Merchant Aircraft Carriers, as they were called, were to be tankers or bulk grain carriers. They would have a proper flight deck and carry three or four Swordfish aircraft armed with either rockets or depth charges. The nineteen ships that were converted still carried their normal cargoes, which were piped into the holds. *H.M.S. Pretoria Castle* was the training base for the pilots on these new escort carriers. It was intended to convert both the *Dunnottar Castle* and the *Carnarvon Castle* as well to be Aircraft Carriers but the Admiralty changed their minds and both liners became troopships instead.

It was in 1942 that the war reached its peak in the Atlantic. By now Germany was able to keep one hundred submarines at sea at the same time and this was reflected in the number of sinkings. Throughout 1942 the average was one hundred ships a month being sunk. In June alone the total ships sunk amounted to 144… almost five a day. It was at this time that small aircraft carriers (converted merchant ships), were introduced. By 1943 the effects of this and new other new weapons had reduced the losses and the number of submarines sunk rose dramatically.

By 1942 the Axis powers had control of most of the Mediterranean as they had now advanced along the North African coast and were deep into Egypt. Their main concern was the island of Malta, which straddled the shipping routes and was a constant threat to the German and Italian supply lines. They decided that Malta should be heavily attacked to try and force the island to surrender. During 1942 the island dockyards were severely damaged and food and other supplies became scarce, in particular aviation fuel for the aircraft. A decision was taken that the island had to be supplied at all costs. Many merchant ships and warships were to be sunk in the attempt to bring vital food and war materials to the island.

The most important convoy to set out for Malta was code named 'Pedestal'. It sailed from Britain on the 2nd August 1942 and consisted of fourteen merchant ships, one of which was the *Rochester Castle*. There were several refrigerated cargo ships in the convoy carrying the sorely needed food supplies. The escort for this convoy was two battleships, the *Nelson* and the *Rodney*, two cruisers *Nigeria* and *Manchester* and thirteen destroyers. When the convoy approached Gibraltar this armada was increased by three aircraft carriers *Indomitable*, *Victorious* and *Eagle*, three additional cruisers and around twenty more destroyers. Never were so few defended by so many. It certainly indicates how important it was that at least some of these ships got through. Once the convoy passed through the Straits of Gibraltar, the first threat was likely to come from the aircraft based on Sardinia and Sicily. Certainly it was not long before enemy aircraft were shadowing the convoy. There was also the threat that the Italian Navy with their battleships might leave port and launch an attack. In addition there were fast E boats with their torpedoes plus the underwater threat from both Italian and German submarines that would be lying in wait for the convoy

The first attack came in the early afternoon of the 11th August. A submarine torpedoed the aircraft carrier *Eagle* and she sank with all her aircraft in just a few minutes. Following this the air attacks started. Waves of aircraft made continuous sorties. The *Rochester Castle*, armed with two Bofors guns and six Oerlikons, was in constant action as were all the ships. She suffered some damage when she suffered some near misses and water began to leak into the engine room. The following day the bombers were back again and in the evening the first merchant ship was lost, hit by an aerial torpedo. During the day more ships were sunk including two of the escorts. A Clan Line ship immediately astern of the *Rochester Castle* received a direct hit and blew up as she was carrying high-octane fuel. During the night the *Rochester Castle* was hit near the number 3 hatch by a torpedo fired from an E boat. The hold filled with water and the ship was down by the head. She still managed to maintain her speed at around 13 knots. At daybreak dive-bombers attacked and more ships were sunk. Again the ship astern of the *Rochester Castle* received a direct hit and blew up. The *Rochester Castle* was also damaged and was on fire. By now both her forward holds were leaking and the water was rising despite the pumps. In the early evening the *Rochester Castle* was the first of the surviving merchant ships to limp into the Grand Harbour at Valetta. The *Rochester Castle* was given temporary repairs in the Naval dockyards and she remained at Malta until December. She then left Malta and sailed to New York via Cape Town where permanent repairs were carried out.

It was perhaps at the end of 1942 that the tide of war started to turn in favour of the Allies. This was when the landings by Allied Forces took place in North Africa. The *Durban Castle* was the Headquarters ship for the invasion fleet and also present were the *Winchester Castle, Warwick Castle, Arundel Castle* and the *Llangibby Castle*. The landings began in the early morning of the 8th November 1942. Early on, the *Llangibby Castle* received a direct hit from one of the shore batteries. She fired back with her own six-inch guns and after several salvos the battery was silenced. Algiers and Oran were soon overrun and the troopships having played their part were no longer required. The liners headed back to Gibraltar where they arrived safely with the exception of the *Viceroy of India*, which was sunk. When the convoy sailed back to England the *Warwick Castle*, which was at the rear of the convoy, was hit by a torpedo. She sank in less than an hour and a half but because of the bad weather conditions it took six hours to rescue all the survivors. Several months later the *Windsor Castle* was also carrying troops to Algiers when an aerial torpedo hit her. It was decided to abandon the ship and this time the weather was good and the troops were taken on board the Naval ships that were standing by. Some of the crew remained on board, but about six hours later it was decided to take the crew off. It was then decided to try and take the *Windsor Castle* in tow and the Captain and a skeleton crew went back on board. However, the Captain soon realised that the ship was about to sink. Everyone was taken off just in time before she sank by the stern.

The next landings to take place in July 1943 were on the island of Sicily. The *Llangibby Castle* was involved again carrying the Canadian commandos and the *Durban Castle* was present as well with a contingent of Marine commandos. The *Winchester Castle* carried two thousand men of the 8th Army from Egypt to take part. Both the *Winchester Castle* and the *Durban Castle* were present again when the first landings took place on mainland Europe at Salerno and Anzio.

By this time the *Llangibby Castle* was back in the dockyard being converted into an Infantry Landing Ship with eighteen landing craft. She took part in the 'D' Day landings in Normandy with a contingent from the Royal Marine Flotilla to man her landing craft. She landed the Canadian troops on board in the first wave. Later as the weather worsened ten of her landing craft capsized and twelve men were drowned. The *Llangibby Castle* continued to carry troops across the Channel and altogether she made seventy crossings, carrying in total around 100,000 men. The *Llandovery Castle,* as a hospital ship also took part in this campaign and she shuttled between Cherbourg and Southampton. On one voyage she took wounded Canadian troops back to Montreal.

Also on 'D' Day the *Winchester Castle* and the *Durban Castle* were occupied elsewhere. They were taking part in Operation Dragoon in the Mediterranean, disembarking troops on the Cote d'Azur in the South of France.

In the latter part of the war the *Llanstephan Castle* was taken over by the Royal Indian Navy as a troopship. She was converted to an Infantry Landing Ship with eighteen landing craft and was used in the Dutch East Indies, still manned by Indian personnel. The *Llangibby Castle* in 1945 carried troops to the Far East. Then she was involved when the war ended in repatriating 6,000 West African troops from Burma and India. It took three voyages and she was away for twelve months. It was the longest recorded voyage from Southampton and back in the history of the Company. On one voyage she carried a complete military prison.

When the war came to an end in 1945 the Union-Castle fleet had suffered thirteen losses. The worst year was 1942 when five of the Company's ships were sunk. Of the mail ships six remained and there were also six intermediate liners. Of the refrigerated cargo vessels three had been sunk. In February 1942 the *Rowallan Castle* was in a convoy that sailed from Alexandria en route to Malta. When German aircraft attacked the convoy, the *Rowallan Castle* was hit. *H.M.S. Zulu* took her in tow, but when it became clear that there was no hope of saving her, she was sunk by gunfire. Prior to this the *Rowallan Castle* had been lucky to survive 'friendly fire'. She was close to the Azores at night when she failed to respond to signals made by the Armed Merchant Cruiser *Circassia.* The *Rowallan Castle* instead altered course and opened fire. This brought several broadsides from the *Circassia.* She then signalled again and the *Rowallan Castle* responded this time. She had been damaged but was able to proceed on her voyage. More often than not the 'R' boats, because of their speed, did not join in convoys, they operated on their own.

Her sister ship the *Richmond Castle* was lost later the same year when she was torpedoed in the North Atlantic by a German submarine. In 1943 the

Roxburgh Castle, having survived being bombed twice while she was in Liverpool, was also torpedoed and sunk close to the Azores. The only survivor of this class was the *Rochester Castle*. The Company retained her until 1970 when she was finally scrapped. She had the longest career of any of the Company's cargo boats of just on thirty-three years. For the second time in just over twenty-five years the Union-Castle Company were faced with a substantial building programme to replace the ships that had been lost.

The Sea Front, Durban

CHAPTER 7 - THE END OF THE LINE

As the war drew to a close, firstly in Europe and then a few months later in the Far East, so the work began to restore Union-Castle's normal services as quickly as possible. It was obvious that it would take some time, as the passenger ships would be required to transport millions of servicemen, which included those that were sick or wounded, back to their home countries. In addition there were also hundreds of thousands of prisoners of war to be repatriated, not to mention untold numbers of displaced persons. In the event it all took much longer than anyone had anticipated.

Like all the shipping companies, Union-Castle had lost a number of ships during the war. In the first instance two new mail ships would be needed for the two that had been lost. Two 28,000-ton replacements were soon ordered from Harland & Wolff's shipyards in Belfast. Of the intermediate fleet the *Dunvegan Castle*, *Dunbar Castle*, *Llandaff Castle* and the *Gloucester Castle* had all been lost. The last named had been due to be scrapped in 1939 but replacements for the others would soon be required. In addition some of the older liners would be going for scrap within a few years. During the war some replacements had been built. Three new refrigerated cargo vessels had joined the fleet to replace those that had been lost. They were in fact given the same names *Rowallan Castle*, *Richmond Castle*, and *Roxburgh Castle*. They were very similar to their predecessors, though were slightly larger and a knot faster. The first to appear was the *Rowallan Castle* in 1943 and the other two appeared in the following year. At the very end of the war in Europe the *Riebeck Castle* also joined the fleet, to be followed three months later by the *Rustenburg Castle*. Of the general cargo boats only the *Sandown Castle* remained plus the Beira based coaster, the *Rovuma*. Both of these were getting old and the *Rovuma* was sold in 1949. The *Sandown Castle*, after twenty-nine years, was first laid up in early 1950 and was then sent to the breakers later that same year.

M.V. Rustenburg Castle. 1946 -1971. 8,322 gross tons. A refrigerated fruit ship.

One of the first of the intermediates to be returned to normal service was the *Llandovery Castle* and the people on board had a most odd experience. On the 1st July 1947 she was steaming through the Straits of Madagascar. At about 11 p.m. some of the passengers were on deck and noticed a bright light over the ship. This light went ahead of the *Llandovery Castle* and lost height and speed until it was about fifty feet above the water. The light was now abeam of the ship and when it was put out, both passengers and crew could see a very large metallic looking craft some one thousand feet long. It was shaped like a cigar with one end clipped. It had no visible windows or portholes and appeared to be about 200 feet wide. It cruised alongside the ship for about a minute before silently rising to about a thousand feet. Then the craft emitted streams of orange flames before shooting upwards and disappearing into the night. An entry of this sighting was made in the ship's log.

In that post war era many ports around the world became congested. As far as Union-Castle were concerned the main port that became a problem was Beira, with both intermediate liners and cargo ships being delayed. The port itself lies partly below sea level and it is both very hot and humid. When the liners were anchored off, only Portuguese launches could be used to ferry passengers ashore and this was very expensive. Those who did go ashore found that there was not a lot to do or see. The port only had five berths and Portuguese ships took preference. This meant that a stay of up to seven days was not unusual for the intermediates, and much, much longer for the Company's cargo boats.

S.S. Good Hope Castle 1947 - 1959. 9,905 gross tons. Seen here berthed in the Royal Albert Dock in 1952.

The Company had decided in 1946 that they needed to introduce new general cargo ships. Under the Government scheme for the disposal of ships after the war had ended, Union-Castle first took over the _Empire Life_ and renamed her _Good Hope Castle_. She was unusual in that she had accommodation for fifty-four passengers and her gross tonnage was 9,879. The second ship they acquired was the _Drakensberg Castle_, previously the _Empire Allenby_. She was slightly larger but had accommodation for only thirty-six passengers. Finally the _Kenilworth Castle_ (formerly the _Empire Wilson_) joined the fleet, again slightly larger and also capable of carrying thirty-six passengers. All of these were designated as fast cargo liners and were capable of fifteen knots. The number of passengers carried was later reduced to the more normal twelve on all three ships.

Three years later a further cargo vessel was purchased. She was originally named the _Empire Duchess_ and had been under Union-Castle management since 1946. However, in 1950 the Company purchased the vessel and renamed her _Braemar Castle_. In the following year she was transferred to King Line, which was a subsidiary of Union-Castle, and renamed _King James_.

In the immediate post war period fares in general had risen. The cost of the Round Africa trip of some nine or ten weeks had increased substantially. To take the _Dunnottar Castle_ as an example the First Class fares varied from £300 to £210. The fares for passengers sailing on the older ships were slightly less. The Tourist Class rates at the time ranged from £152 to £136. It is likely that anyone booking for the entire voyage would have received a fairly substantial discount, dependent on whether the ship was full.

The _Llanstephan Castle_ may have gone through two world wars unscathed, but she was soon in trouble on her return to the Company. In the early 1950's she arrived at St. Helena and dropped her port anchor, which disappeared with a rush together with the chain. She then dropped her starboard anchor, which also disappeared down the same hole. When she arrived in Cape Town she looked rather odd with no anchors at all.

As part of the new mail contract that had been negotiated as the war drew to a close, two of the Company's cargo boats were to be registered in South Africa. The first to be transferred was the _Good Hope Castle_ on the 14th July 1946 and shortly afterwards the _Drakensberg Castle_ was also placed on the South African Register. Initially all the cargo boats were given lavender hulls but in 1953 this was changed to black which had been the colour before the war. It was a refrigerated cargo vessel, the _Roxburgh Castle_ that resumed the mail service by taking the first sailing on the 2nd January 1947, and four days later the _Riebeck Castle_ took the first mail sailing from Cape Town. The following week the _Capetown Castle_, the commodore ship, became the first liner to return to the mail run. As time went on so more of the liners were refurbished and returned to the fleet, but were not necessarily placed on their normal routes. The *Durban Castle* and the *Warwick Castle* were amongst the first of the liners to be released and they were placed on the mail run and did not rejoin the Round Africa service for some long time. The *Warwick Castle* was originally the *Pretoria Castle,* but her name was changed as one of the two new mail ships was to be called *Pretoria Castle.* It was not until 1950 that the last mail ship, the *Arundel Castle* returned to the mail service, almost five years after the war ended.

In April 1948 the new Union-Castle brochure listed all the ships that remained in the fleet, but of course at that time quite a number had not yet been returned to the Company. In addition the ports of call listed for the Round Africa service still reflected the pre-war situation. Included were calls in the Mediterranean at Tangier and Palma, Majorca. It may well be that at the time the intention was to resume these calls, but in fact this never happened. Calls at Port Amelia and Mozambique in Portuguese East Africa were still on the schedule and these did occur but at irregular intervals. The Intermediate service to Beira was the same, as both Reunion and Mauritius were included, but regular calls were never reinstated. Tenerife was also included as an alternative call instead of Las Palmas, but by the next printing of the brochure, this too had been deleted. At this time only three liners were operating on the Round Africa run and there was a considerable demand for both berths and cargo space.

It had been originally hoped that the mail service would be back to normal by 1948, but the *Carnarvon Castle, Winchester Castle,* and *Arundel Castle* had been retained to carry emigrants to South Africa and this went on until 1949, far longer than had been anticipated. The problem was the large number of emigrants who wanted to take passage to South Africa. Many soldiers and others from the armed services had visited either Cape Town or Durban on their way to Egypt, and later the Far East during the war, and perhaps liked what they saw. To start with emigrants could get assisted passages although this was stopped later on. There was something of a post war boom in South Africa, which affected both Southern and Northern Rhodesia. On the East coast as well, the groundnut scheme in Tanganyika, also attracted many immigrants although by the early 1950's this project had been abandoned. In South Africa they discovered gold in the Orange Free State, and also in the country as a whole there was a shortage of tradesmen and technicians. In the beginning the previous government sponsored suitable candidates to emigrate with jobs guaranteed. The three liners, between them, carried around 32,000 emigrants to South Africa before they were released back to the company. They then had to be refurbished before they could join the mail service.

In addition to these difficulties there were other delaying factors, in the immediate years following the war. Shipbuilding costs were up substantially and also the pound sterling had been devalued. This meant that the costs of building and operating the liners were also much higher than before the war.

Added to that, were the rising maintenance costs plus congestion in some of the ports that caused long delays. The mail ships were seldom if ever delayed because of the mail contract. In the same way the Round Africa liners also carried the mails for Kenya, Tanganyika and Uganda and in the main were not affected by congestion, although occasional delays did occur in Portuguese East Africa. The demand for cargo space for freight to East Africa was so high that long delays in delivery were inevitable. Many smaller items in demand, such as clothing and shoes were sent instead by registered post, as there were no delays with the mail.

The problems on the mail service prior to the end of 1950 had a knock on effect with the Round Africa service. From 1947 first the *Llangibby Castle* and then the *Llanstephan Castle* joined the *Llandovery Castle* on the route, but the next ship to rejoin, after a ten month refit, was the *Dunnottar Castle* in February 1949 more than a year later. Even then there was still a very skimpy service compared with pre-war. Nine ships had been on the run of which three had been lost. However, the *Durban Castle* and the *Warwick Castle* were still to come to complete the planned service, with three ships going out by the West Coast, and three going out via Suez. A further problem was the age of the three older liners. In particular the *Llanstephan Castle*, which sailed on her maiden voyage in 1914 and by 1949 was already thirty-five years old. The *Llandovery Castle* was twenty-four years old and the *Llangibby Castle* had made her maiden voyage in 1929.

The next ship to appear after the new mail ships, *Pretoria Castle and Edinburgh Castle* was the *Bloemfontein Castle*. She was the largest intermediate the Company had ever built at 18,400 gross tons, and she was also the first one class ship. In addition she was the first Union-Castle liner to have only the one mast. She was built to cater for the anticipated rush of emigrants to Southern and East Africa. She carried 725 passengers in one, two, and three berth cabins, with a few four berths. The dining saloon could not hold all the passengers so there were two sittings for meals.

The normal 'shakedown cruise' on the *Bloemfontein Castle*, when she left Harland and Wolff's Belfast shipyard, was not quite the same as it had been in the past. She had on board the usual invited guests of the Company, but in this instance it was 250 members of staff from Union-Castle offices in London and Southampton. It was quite an experience for many, who although working for a shipping company, never had an opportunity to set foot on one of the Company's liners, let alone sail on one. It was a great success and the voyage, albeit short, was enjoyed by everyone without exception.

Bloemfontein Castle sailed on her maiden voyage shortly afterwards on the 6th April 1950 with a full complement of over seven hundred passengers. Although she had been intended for the Intermediate service to Beira, her first voyage was on the Round Africa run, going out via the Cape and returning through the Suez Canal. It had been the intention originally to place her permanently on the Round Africa run, but because of the failure of the groundnuts scheme in Tanganyika, she was placed on the Beira run instead.

The *Bloemfontein Castle* broke down on her maiden voyage off the West Coast of Africa when she had a total failure of her generators. One after another they all failed until the ship was dead in the water roughly 500 miles from Walvis Bay. The engine room staff took some time to get the ship underway again and she eventually arrived in Cape Town late. When she returned to London at the end of the voyage the Company decided that all the generators should be replaced. When the *Bloemfontein Castle* arrived in Cape Town a special luncheon was held on board the ship on the 24th April. The host, on behalf of the Company, was Mr. R.M.Mackenzie, the Chief Agent for Union-Castle for South and East Africa.. The principal guest was the South African Minister of Economic Affairs, the Honourable E.H. Louw. When the ship reached Durban, the ship's company played host to several hundred school children who had come down for the day from the City of Bloemfontein. They explored the ship from stem to stern and enjoyed a special luncheon before setting off back home.

M.V. Bloemfontein Castle 1950 - 1959. 18,400 gross tons. Made one voyage around Africa and was then placed on the Beira run.

After her maiden voyage the *Bloemfontein Castle* joined the London – Rotterdam –Cape Town – Beira service. She also called at Las Palmas, Lobito Bay and Walvis Bay outward bound, followed by the Cape ports and Lourenco Marques. She returned by the same route usually missing out the call at Lobito Bay. She did not always call at Rotterdam on the outward voyage it depended

120

whether there were German passengers on their way to settle in what had been German South West Africa prior to the First World War.

The *Bloemfontein Castle* was not destined to be the luckiest of ships. On a later voyage she again broke down, once more in the South Atlantic when she had a problem with one of her main engines, which had to be shut down. When she got underway again she was running on one engine and she limped into Cape Town late. Many passengers complained about the terrible vibration because she had been operating flat out on the one engine so as not to lose too much time.

Her trips up and down the coast to Beira and back became very popular in the South African holiday season. The most popular destination at the time was Lorenco Marques. However, it was not very long before the *Bloemfontein Castle* was in trouble once more, this time in Beira. She was just on the point of sailing down the coast for Lourenco Marques. The gangway had been taken away and the lines had been singled up, when somehow or other a wrong valve was opened and water flooded in to the engine room. The starter motors for the main engines were low down and the seawater covered them causing them to burn out. There was no other way to start the main engines. The armatures from the motors had to be flown back to England to be rewound and it was several days before they were returned and the *Bloemfontein Castle* could sail on her way. Because of all her teething problems she was given the name 'Bedlam Castle'. The final disaster for the ship was the rapid decline in emigrants going to South Africa. The main factor, that caused this traffic to South Africa in particular, to dry up was the result of the general election in 1948. This was when Dr. Malan's National Party defeated the United Party led by Field Marshal Smuts. In due course this brought about the end of the assisted passage scheme to South Africa. It later also brought about the sale of the ship after only nine years in service.

Shortly after the *Bloemfontein Castle* joined the fleet, it was announced that three more one-class vessels were to be ordered for the Round Africa service. They were to be much the same as the *Bloemfontein Castle* but slightly smaller and would have the traditional two masts. It is likely that they were similar in tonnage to the pre-war *Durban Castle* and *Warwick Castle*. They could enter the port of Dar-es-Salaam but the *Bloemfontein Castle* could not. The first two ships were built with accommodation for 530 passengers where as the last to appear had twenty-six more berths, as the Clubroom, a feature of the other two ships, was replaced with more cabins. The grades of the cabins were mainly Cabin Class, so this was an improvement on the *Bloemfontein Castle*, which was really only Tourist Class although the better cabins were graded cabin class. The new ships also had limited air conditioning in the shop, the hairdressing salon, the ship's hospital and the dining saloon. This was a considerable boon in the heat of the Red Sea and the East Coast. The three

121

ships in order of appearance were named *Rhodesia Castle*, *Kenya Castle* and *Braemar Castle*. All of them were just over 17,000 gross tons with a speed of more than 17 knots. Together with the *Warwick Castle* and *Durban Castle* these were the largest ships to enter Dar-es-Salaam and they were moored in the harbour in a special way so that they would not swing. The stern of the ship was tied up to the shore and forward both anchors were dropped. This meant that the ship could not swing with the changes in the wind direction and the tides.

THE DOCKHEAD.   SOUTHAMPTON.   9166.

Southampton Docks circa 1950. Showing the Durban Castle and Warwick Castle.

Perhaps the *Bloemfontein Castle's* finest hour came on the 8th January 1953. The Dutch liner *Klipfontein* struck an uncharted rock about one hundred miles North of Lourenco Marques. She had departed from Durban the previous day after embarking her passengers and loading a cargo of manganese ore. She was on her way to Holland via the Suez Canal. She was in a hurry as her next port of call, Beira was very congested and there was only the one berth available. She was hoping to get to Beira to claim that berth before the *Bloemfontein Castle* so that she would not lose time. After striking the rock the *Klipfontein* began to settle by the head and an oil tank exploded in the bows, fortunately without anyone being hurt. The captain then decided to abandon ship. A distress call went out over the radio that was picked up by the *Bloemfontein Castle* coming up from the South at full speed. There was plenty of time to get all the passengers into the boats. However, many had lost all their baggage, together with their passports, papers and valuables. The problem had

122

been that some of the cabins had been quickly flooded and in addition the ship's safe in the Purser's office had been cut off by rising water. By two o'clock, only forty minutes after the *Klipfontein* had struck, the *Bloemfontein Castle* arrived on the scene and was soon using her motor launch to bring the lifeboats alongside the ship.

In a remarkable short space of time all 233 passengers and crew were safely on board. The *Klipfontein* remained afloat until four o'clock when she sank and the *Bloemfontein Castle* then carried on to Beira. At Beira, the agents for the *Klipfontein* had booked all the available accommodation for the passengers and crew. Fortunately the passengers were able to resume their journey on another ship the following day.

There was another outing for the staff of the London office in October 1951. This came when the Chairman, Sir Vernon Thompson, now in his seventies, invited everyone to tea on board the *Rhodesia Castle* while she was lying in the King George V Dock in London. The visit was arranged for a Saturday afternoon when coaches were laid on to bring the staff from the City to the ship when the office closed at lunchtime. The splendid tea was another resounding success and once more gave the Company's employees an opportunity to have a good look round the public rooms, cabins, engine room and the bridge.

With the arrival of the *Rhodesia Castle* on the Round Africa run, the *Llanstephan Castle* was withdrawn and went for scrap. She had the longest career of all the Union-Castle ships, and her paying off pennant was over two hundred feet long. The three one class vessels, although no one realised it at the time, were the last to be built for the Round Africa service.

The *Kenya Castle*, the second of the three vessels, arrived in Southampton on the 18th February 1952. On the 7th March she set off on a two week cruise calling at Lisbon, Las Palmas, Casablanca, Malaga and Cadiz. She returned to London and sailed from there on her first Round Africa voyage. When she reached Zanzibar, she was visited by the Sultan Kalif bin Harab and his wife the Sultana. He was particularly interested in seeing the image of Zanzibar, and the ships nearby on the radar screen on the bridge of the vessel. The arrival of the two new intermediates on the Round Africa run caused some changes in the schedule. As a result the *Warwick Castle* did three one-week cruises in November and December 1952, calling at Spanish and North African ports.

The final ship, the *Braemar Castle* entered the service on the 20th November 1952. There were now six modern ships circumnavigating Africa on a voyage lasting just under ten weeks. There were two sailings a month from London, one via the West Coast and the other via the Mediterranean and the Suez Canal. These two ships replaced the *Llandovery Castle* and the *Llangibby Castle*. They both temporarily joined the *Bloemfontein Castle* on the intermediate service to Beira. The *Llandovery Castle* was sent to the breakers in 1953 and the *Llangibby Castle* followed in 1954.

The sudden and unexpected death of Sir Vernon Thompson in January 1953, just before the Company celebrated its one hundredth anniversary, created major problems. Like Sir Donald Currie before him, Sir Vernon Thompson had kept the reins of control in his own hands and consequently there was an enormous gap to be filled when he died. History repeated itself, in that within a comparatively short time the Company was merged with the Clan Line under the umbrella of the British & Commonwealth Shipping Company Limited. The merger was effective as from the 31st January 1956.

On the 7th October 1953 the Union-Castle Line celebrated its centenary. In 1853 when the Union Line had been founded there had been just five ships with a total gross tonnage of 2,237. One hundred years later the Company operated a fleet of twenty-six ships with a total tonnage of 411,000.

Following the war the exports of fruit from South Africa had declined when compared with shipments in the late 1930's. It was mostly due to the fact that neither the passenger liners nor all the refrigerated cargo vessels were all back to normal service until 1950. Soon after this the pre-war export totals were being exceeded. Shipments of deciduous fruits amounted to more than five million packages with citrus fruits at just over four million. Ten years later the advance had continued with seven million packages of deciduous fruits but the amount of citrus fruit had fallen slightly to just over four million. By this time the range of fruits exported had widened, and bulk shipments of wine and fruit juices were growing rapidly.

By 1972 the total number of packages of fruit shipped to the United Kingdom had reached a total of thirteen million. Union-Castle at this time were employing nine refrigerated cargo ships plus all the mail ships were carrying large quantities of fruit in their cold chambers. Even the fast cargo ships which were used on the mail run, the *Good Hope Castle* and the *Southampton Castle* both had a 60,000 gallon tank for carrying wine.

In 1954 two new general cargo ships had joined the fleet. They were the first to be built for the Company for many years. They were both 7,448 gross tons and had a speed of sixteen knots. They also had accommodation for twelve passengers. The *Tantallon Castle* was the first of the two to appear when she sailed on her maiden voyage in March 1954. Her sister ship, the *Tintagel Castle* left London on her first voyage in June the same year. They were both employed initially on the South Africa – U.S. –U.K. service. The *Tintagel Castle* was in fact the last cargo ship to be built for the Line.

In 1955 the merger between the Union-Castle Mail Steamship Company Limited and Clan Line Steamers Limited was announced on October 5th. The actual merger took place on 31st January 1956. The shares of the two companies were to be acquired by a holding Company, the British and Commonwealth Shipping Company Limited. Following the merger of Union-Castle and Clan Line the combined fleets of the two companies amounted to ninety nine ships with one being built, the Pendennis Castle which had been laid down at Harland and Wolff's yard in November 1955. In August 1956 the new Company ordered two refrigerated cargo vessels from the Greenock Dockyard Company. The first of these was the *Rotherwick Castle*, which sailed from Middlesborough on her first voyage on the 30th December 1959 bound for Beira. Her sister ship the *Rothesay Castle* sailed on her first voyage from Hamburg on the 31st July 1960 bound for Cape Town. Both ships had a gross tonnage of 9,360 and a speed of seventeen knots.

M.V. Tintagel Castle. 1954 - 1971. 7,447 gross tons. The last general cargo vessel to be built by Union-Castle.

The closure of the Suez Canal in 1956 because of the 'Six Days War' disrupted the Round Africa service but fortunately it was not too long before the canal was re-opened. At Port Said the departure time of the south bound convoy through the Canal was always governed by the time the convoy from Suez arrived. Carrying the Royal Mail did have its advantages as this meant a place at or near the head of the convoy. You could therefore leave the Canal at Suez a couple of hours earlier than might have otherwise been the case.

The route and ports of call of the Round Africa ships attracted several travel writers in the 1950's and 1960's. The most eminent of these was Evelyn Waugh who wrote the book 'A Tourist in Africa'. He travelled by train from London to Genoa and boarded the *Rhodesia Castle* there at the end of January 1959. He left the ship at Dar-es-Salaam and then spent five weeks visiting different countries in Africa before joining the *Pendennis Castle* at Cape Town for the homeward voyage. He was very pleased with the range of books that were carried in the Library on both vessels. S.P.B. Mais did much the same thing a year later. He in fact also travelled on the *Rhodesia Castle* but went all the way to Durban. He then transferred to the *Pendennis Castle* for the voyage back to England. His book was titled *'Round Africa Cruise Holiday'*. Earlier J.Allan Cash, the well-known photographer, sailed around Africa on the *Kenya Castle*. His main purpose was taking photographs, many of which were used at the time in the Company's brochures. He did in fact in 1955 also write a book, incorporating many of his photographs titled *'African Voyage'*.

It had become obvious by the second half of the 1950's that momentous changes were about to occur in Africa. The old colonies of the European powers were slowly but surely edging their way towards independence. This inevitably would affect Union-Castle, specifically the Round Africa service. The bulk of the passengers travelling in these ships were colonial civil servants who enjoyed a long home leave at regular intervals in the United Kingdom. As independence was given to the different countries so most of these civil servants would be replaced. Those that were retained would not have the same generous conditions as before and, in all probability with shorter home leave, they would travel by air and not by sea. The first casualty as a result of the changes came in 1958 when the *Dunnottar Castle* was the first of the Round Africa vessels to be considered surplus to requirements and she was sold.

It was necessary, following the departure of the *Dunnottar Castle*, to re-schedule the remaining liners. This meant that the *Rhodesia Castle* would be idle for several weeks. It was decided therefore that she should make two cruises each lasting ten days, calling at four Ports, Malaga, Gibraltar, Casablanca and Lisbon. Some extra staff were brought in which included an Entertainments Officer, a four-piece dance band, two travel agents to organise the shore excursions and a photographer. The two cruises were well publicised in the press and in addition, a prize of two free tickets was won on the then popular television Quiz programme *'Take your Pick'*, presented by Michael Miles. This gave added publicity and the cruises were a success

The luckless *Bloemfontein Castle* was sold the following year. Her last voyage from Cape Town was a fair indication of the problem as she only had on board sixty-eight passengers travelling back to England. Looking at the Round Africa ships at around the same time, the fall in passenger numbers was not all that apparent, certainly not in the sailings from London. Taking some outward voyages as an example during the 1950's and early 1960's:-

16/9/1958	*Warwick Castle*	ex London via Suez	90% full
26/10/1960	*Rhodesia Castle*	ex London via Suez	100% full
28/ 8/1953	*Durban Castle*	ex London via Suez	82% full
1/9/1955	*Braemar Castle*	ex London via Cape Town	75% full
16/ 9/1953	*Warwick Castle*	ex London via Cape Town	90% full

These figures exclude passengers from London disembarking at the Mediterranean ports. In the summer months this could be a substantial number. As a whole the figures for the liners going out via Suez in particular, seem fairly consistent. Via Cape Town there was more competition from other liners of course, not forgetting the Company's own mail ships. However, after 1960 numbers began to fall rapidly as the switch to air travel gathered speed. By 1962 the Round Africa route ceased and was replaced by the London to Durban via Suez service which lasted until 1967. The figures above were obtained from the printed passenger lists. It is significant that after 1960 these are very hard to find.

The *Drakensberg Castle* was sold in 1959 to be broken up in Hong Kong. Prior to her voyage to the breaker's yard, the *Drakensberg Castle* was lucky to survive a serious fire in Newcastle docks. Berthed alongside, having partly offloaded a cargo of highly flammable sisal, suddenly a fire started in one of the sheds, which spread with frightening speed. This meant that the *Drakensberg Castle* was in a very dangerous position. The fire was so fierce that members of the deck crew risked the intense heat and went ashore to cast off her moorings. This allowed the ship to drift away from the quayside. Tugs then took her in tow and moved her out of the danger zone. It took six fire engines to get the flames under control and the damage done to the wharf and sheds was considerable. The *Drakensberg Castle* was able to complete discharging her cargo of sisal two days later.

Her last voyage to Hong Kong was also incident filled. Having loaded cargo for Shanghai she left Antwerp on the 16th June. Initially she had engine trouble and at one point was adrift off Cherbourg. The problem was sorted out and she sailed through the Mediterranean and reached Port Said on the 27th June. In the Red Sea the engines failed again and she did not arrive in Aden until the third of July. She sailed three days later into bad weather and because of this, one of the crew was injured. As a result the ship had to turn round and go back to Aden where the seaman was taken to hospital. The *Drakensberg Castle* sailed on the following day and arrived in Singapore on the 19th July. Just over a week later she reached Shanghai and by the 1st August all the cargo had been discharged. She then sailed for her final destination, Hong Kong, where she berthed on the 5th August. Two days later the crew flew back to England via Karachi and Nicosia.

The older colonies were the first to gain their independence, mostly on the Western side of Africa. In 1960 these included Ghana (formerly the Gold Coast), the Belgian Congo, Ivory Coast and Somalia. The following year Tanganyka gained independence, as did Malawi (previously Nyasaland) which became a self governing Protectorate, gaining full independence in 1964. Also, in the same year, both Kenya and Zanzibar became self-governing and later the same year so did Zambia (formerly Northern Rhodesia).

Following the departure of the *Dunnottar Castle* the number of vessels left on the Round Africa run fell to five. Of these, two sailed out via the Cape and the other three via Suez. For a period the number was reduced to four when the *Braemar Castle* replaced the *Edinburgh Castle* on the mail service when a fire in Southampton damaged her.

Between 1957 and 1960 some alterations were made to the ships in the fleet. First of all the teak masts on the liners were painted white. Shortly afterwards, in turn the three one class vessels were taken out of service when each ship had its funnel heightened and a dome top fitted. This was done to reduce the likelihood of smoke and smuts being blown down onto the after passenger decks. In addition the passenger accommodation was up-graded creating more cabins with en-suite baths or showers. In some cases, air conditioning was introduced for the top grade cabins. Altogether, the result was a reduction in the number of passengers carried. On the *Rhodesia Castle* and *Kenya Castle* the numbers fell to 442 and on the *Braemar Castle* to 459. Following the explosion in the engine room on the *Capetown Castle* on the 17th October 1960, some of the passengers and crew were transferred to the *Braemar Castle*. The *Rowallan Castle* took over the mail sailing while the Capetown Castle was being repaired.

The Bosun of the Kenya Castle supervises the transfer of a crate of lager to the Royal Marine Band on H.M.S. Kenya.
They had given a concert for all on board while both ships were steaming at 17 knots.

In 1961 the _Braemar Castle_ made two cruises to the Eastern Mediterranean, one in the spring and the other in the autumn. Shortly afterwards it was announced that the _Durban Castle_ and _Warwick Castle would_ be withdrawn in 1962. The _Durban Castle_ arrived back in London on the 28th March and was sold for scrap. The _Warwick Castle_ followed in July when she went to be broken up in Barcelona.

A Warwick Castle passenger list showing the Braemar Castle at Zanzibar. Also used as an advertising Poster.

UNION-CASTLE LINE

A Union-Castle Intermediate Vessel at Zanzibar

LIST OF PASSENGERS

M.V. "WARWICK CASTLE"

From London 16th September, 1958

In fact, the _Warwick Castle_ made the last sailing on the Round Africa Service. The new service that replaced it was described as the 'Intermediate East Coast Service'. It was virtually a reversion back to the service that existed prior to 1922. The three one class ships, at monthly intervals, all sailed out via Suez terminating at Durban. They then returned to London via the same route. It was still possible to travel around Africa but it meant that passengers had to transfer to a mail ship at Durban. Both the intermediates and the mail ships arrived on a Tuesday and departed again on Thursday. The round trip for the intermediates was much the same length as before, around sixty-six days. The schedule though was tighter because of the 'rendezvous' with the mail boat at

Durban. They could not afford to be more than two days late.

The ports of call were not quite the same as before, nor was the duration of the time spent in some of the ports. Outward-bound Marseilles had been dropped as well as Port Sudan and Lorenco Marques was now an irregular call. Homeward bound a call was made at Lourenco Marques every other voyage combined with alternating calls at Marseilles and Naples. Less time was now spent in some of the ports. For example the normal stay in Mombasa had been about six days but this had been reduced to three. Once a year one of the intermediates did make a Round Africa voyage, sailing out via the Mediterranean. This was in January, which traditionally had always been the most popular time for both British and American passengers to go on this trip. The Company did draw to the attention of passengers that the vessels might not be in port long enough in some cases, to carry out the shore excursions that were publicised. It was also made clear that ships operating on this service were not engaged on what was commonly known as 'cruising', but on a normal commercial voyage. *'Although every effort would be made to adhere to the provisional printed schedule, occasions may arise, due to cargo requirements and other cases beyond the Company's control, when this is not possible'*. This might be for previous delays, that the call was much shorter than scheduled or that the call was made at night. In one instance the *Rhodesia Castle* was a day late arriving in Mombasa but she sailed on schedule, which meant a stay of only two days. This of course affected the trips to the game parks and Kilimanjaro. One of the highlights of the voyage was sailing close to Stromboli and passing through the Straits of Messina. In the past this was virtually always during the daylight hours. From 1962 it was often the case that the passage could be made at night. In one recorded instance a passenger writes that the ship passed Stromboli at three o'clock in the morning and that they saw very little apart from a few lights.

The withdrawal of the *Durban Castle* and the *Warwick Castle* meant that the Company could no longer cope with the heavy demand for cargo space for the East Coast ports. Two Clan Line cargo boats were therefore renamed *Kinpurnie Castle* and *Kinniard Castle* and they were transferred to the East Coast to meet this demand. In the early 1960's the *Braemar Castle* was on the last lap of her voyage, having arrived at Gibraltar with three hundred passengers on board. She ran aground in a gale as her anchors dragged. High seas pounded the ship while three Admiralty tugs waited for the wind to drop. A lull came in the weather and at high tide the tugs refloated her. She later entered the harbour at Gibraltar where divers carried out an inspection of her keel. The Lloyds surveyor was satisfied that the ship could continue her voyage and she sailed for London the following day.

The *Reina del Mar* had been built for the Pacific Steam Navigation Company Limited, in 1956 and she made her maiden voyage from Liverpool to Valparaiso via the Panama Canal. Only seven years later she was withdrawn from this service as it was no longer profitable and she was adapted for cruising. Her cargo holds were converted to provide more passenger accommodation. In addition, amongst other alterations, her forward restaurant was enlarged to seat over 400 people, and a permanent cinema was built on the boat deck. When completed she was able to carry 1,047 passengers. In the summer of 1964 she made a number of cruises mainly to New York and a couple to Montreal. At the end of the summer she came under Union-Castle management, and later was chartered by the Company. When she arrived at Southampton she was repainted in Union-Castle colours and then left for Cape Town to embark on cruises to South America until March 1965.

S.S. Kinpurnie Castle 1962 - 1967. 8,121 gross tons. Transferred to Union-Castle following the end of the Round Africa service

On her return to the Northern hemisphere in the spring, the *Reina del Mar* went on a range of cruises from Southampton, still under Union-Castle management. These started in mid April and went on until early November. The publicity at the time referred to the comfortable cabins, spread over five decks, attentive service and delicious food and spacious decks. In addition, the fact that she had stabilisers and full air conditioning was also mentioned. During the season she made fourteen cruises, mostly in the Western Mediterranean or the Canary Islands, Madeira, Casablanca and Lisbon. The length of the cruises varied between twelve and twenty days. Some of the longer cruises did include calls in the Eastern Mediterranean and the Aegean. Athens, Izmir, Venice and Dubrovnik were amongst the ports of call. The accommodation on the *Reina del Mar* was on five decks and ranged from two berth outer cabins to four berth inners. Altogether there were ten bars on the ship, with the Coral lounge being credited with having the longest bar on any

British ship. The Ocean bar was the most popular with passengers and it stayed open until two o'clock in the morning.

M.V. Reina del Mar 1964 - 1975. 20,263 gross tons. Cruised in the Mediterranean and in the winter cruised out of Cape Town to South America

By early December the *'fabulous Reina del Mar'* (as she was described in the South African advertisements) would be back in Cape Town. She undertook cruises of thirty or so days to Rio de Janeiro, Santos, Buenos Aires and Montevideo. She was also described as *'a one class dreamboat, 182.87 metres of discotheques, swimming pools and bars.'* Also the Ocean bar was said to be the most popular as it stayed open until two o'clock in the morning. *'In addition there were lido's, lounges, restaurants, a cinema and enough deck space to play any game the way you want to'.* She continued to cruise on permanent charter to the Union-Castle Line for a further eight years up to 1973.

In 1965 the *Capetown Castle* was withdrawn from the mail service with the arrival of the *Southampton Castle*. With the speeded up service on the mail run, only five of the liners were retained, all of which could achieve the over 22 knots required. Seven ships were needed to maintain the service and two of the ships were fast cargo vessels, the *Southampton Castle* and the *Good Hope Castle*. They were also to take over the calls at St.Helena and Ascension. The *Southampton Castle* was the first to appear but the *Good Hope Castle* was delayed for some months and the *Capetown Castle* took her sailings. She provided the service to St.Helena and Ascension and was retained for two years as an extra steamer. In May 1966 she went aground at Flushing and it took five tugs to refloat her. Eventually she went to be broken up in 1967.

By 1965 the *Braemar Castle* was engaged in cruising out of Southampton. At the beginning of the following year she was sold for scrap, after only fourteen years in service. This left just the *Rhodesia Castle* and the *Kenya Castle* on the East coast route. An arrangement was made with the British India S.N. Company Limited to operate a joint schedule with their two liners, the *Kenya* and *Uganda*. This meant that there was a three weekly service from London via Suez. In the first half of 1967 both the *Rhodesia Castle* and the *Kenya Castle* were withdrawn. This brought to an end the service to East Africa. The *Kenya Castle* was sold and converted for cruising and the *Rhodesia Castle* was scrapped. The *Kenya Castle* was in fact still cruising up until fairly recently. She has been sold and will become a floating hotel at Canary Wharf. She is coming home as most of her voyages began in the King George V docks. The *Rhodesia Castle* loaded cargo at Rotterdam to be discharged at Bombay, and then she sailed on to Taiwan (formerly Formosa) where she was broken up. The *Stirling Castle* was withdrawn from the mail service in November 1965. In February of the following year she went on two cruises to North African ports. Following this she went to be scrapped.

Before the *Rhodesia Castle* was sold the Company did consider converting her for cruising but decided it would be too costly. However two of the intermediates had long careers as cruise ships, the *Kenya Castle* and the *Dunnottar Castle*. The ex *Transvaal Castle* is still cruising although now around thirty eight years old.

Also in 1967 the *Kinpurnie Castle* made her final voyage. She was still owned by Clan Line but had operated in Union-Castle colours and under their management. She was the last Company vessel to call at Beira on her final voyage before she was sold.

By 1968 the Union Castle fleet had been reduced to three mail ships and two fast cargo boats. Two of the mail ships, *Transvaal Castle* and *Pretoria Castle* had previously been transferred to Safmarine and operated in their colours. The names of the ships respectively were changed to the *S.A. Vaal* and *S.A. Oranje*. Also there were three general cargo boats and eight refrigerated cargo vessels, a total of sixteen ships.

1970/71 had sent six of the refrigerated cargo ships to the breakers. The first to be disposed of was the *Rochester Castle* after, thirty-three years service. In the following year, *Roxburgh Castle*, *Riebeck Castle*, *Rustenberg Castle*, *Richmond Castle* and *Rowallan Castle* had all gone to be broken up.

Towards the end of 1973 the highly popular *Reina del Mar* was purchased by Union-Castle from Royal Mail after they had chartered her for five years. After a few months the company announced that she was to be withdrawn from service in April 1975. The reason given was that the cost of operating her was too high. After a series of cruises to South America from Cape Town, the *Reina del Mar* returned to Southampton and was sent to be scrapped.

It was also in 1975 that the final run down of the Company began. Two of the mail ships, the *Edinburgh Castle* and the *Oranje* (formerly the *Pretoria Castle)* went for scrap. Three cargo vessels were also sold. They were the *Kinniard Castle*, *Rothesay Castle* and the *Rotherwick Castle*. In 1976 the *Pendennis Castle* made her final voyage and was sold in July.

In 1977 four Clan Line cargo vessels were renamed and repainted in Union-Castle colours. They became the *Winchester Castle, Dover Castle, Balmoral Castle* and *Kinpurnie Castle.* It had been announced by then that the two remaining passenger mail ships would be withdrawn in 1977. The *Windsor Castle* made her last voyage from Southampton on the 12th August and the *Vaal* (formerly the *Transvaal Castle*) left on her final voyage on the 2nd September. Both of these ships were sold, the *Windsor Castle* became an accommodation ship in Jeddah and the *Vaal* became a cruise ship. The final sailing on the mail service was taken by the *Southampton Castle*, which left on the 16th September and arrived back on the 24th October. Both the *Good Hope Castle* and the *Southampton Castle* were sold early in 1978.

The only ships that remained now were the four refrigerated cargo vessels, which had been given Union-Castle names previously. In 1979 these four ships were renamed with 'Castle' being dropped and replaced with 'Universal'. In 1981 three more refrigerated cargo boats were bought and put under Union-Castle management. They were the *Caribbean Universal, Edinburgh Universal* and *Stirling Universal.* Effectively though it was the end of the Line and like the old soldier Union-Castle just 'faded away'.

However, in 1998 the Union-Castle Mail Steamship Company Limited rose again. The P.&O. liner, *Victoria* was chartered for a Round Africa voyage, leaving Southampton on the 11th December 1999 and she was in Cape Town for the Millennium celebrations. It is intended that more cruising voyages will be made in the new century.

BIBLIOGRAPHY

Abbott, Peter. The Lavender Hull Mob. Philip Abbott   1995
Bailey J. War Clouds and Honeymoons   Private Publication   1994
Brown A.S. The Guide to South & East Africa. Samson, Low   1936
Cash, Alan.   African Voyage. Fountain Press   1955
Castle Mail Packets - Handbook of Information   1897
Damant H. Every Thursday at 4 o'clock. Overseas Visitors Club   1977
Dunn L. Ships of the Union-Castle Line.   Adlard Coles   1954
Harris C.& Ingpen B. Mailships of the Union Castle Line.
                                            Fernwood Press   1994
Haws D. Merchant Ships in Profile Union-Castle. Patrick Stephens   1990
Haynes A. Union-Castle Line Purserette.   Mallet & Bell   1999
Henzell D. African Patchwork. Newman Neame   1952
Hughes D. & Humphries P. In South African Waters.
                                            Oxford University Press   1977
Knight E. Union-Castle and the War 1914-18. Union Castle   1920
Leathem, Brian. Life with the Castles. Avon Books   1994
Mais S.P.B. Round Africa Cruise Holiday. Alvin Redman   1961
Mallett, Alan. The Union-Castle Line. A Celebration in Photos.
                                            Ship Pictorial Publications 1990
Mitchell W.H. & Sawyer L.A. The Cape Run. Terence Dalton   1984
Murray M. Ships & South Africa. Oxford University Press   1933
Murray M. Union-Castle Chronicle.   Longmans   1953
Newall P. Cape Town Harbour. Portnet.   1993
Newall P. Union-Castle Line. A Fleet History. Carmania Press   1999
Poolman K. Armed Merchant Cruisers. Leo Cooper & Secker   1985
Plumridge Lt.Col. J.H. Hospital Ships and Ambulance Trains.
                                            Seeley Service   1975
Shackleton E.H. & W.McLean. S.S. Tintagel Castle. O.H.M.S.   1900
Steel P.W. In the Shadow of the Hun. Paul Cave Publications   1999
Veitch N. Cape Town Waterfront & Harbour. Human & Rousseau   1994
Waugh Evelyn. A Tourist in Africa. Chapman & Hall Ltd.   1960
Williams D. Liners in Battledress. Conway Maritime Press   1989

NEWSPAPERS AND JOURNALS

BRITISH & COMMONWEALTH REVIEW.
CAPE TIMES, CAPE TOWN.
EASTERN PROVINCE HERALD, PORT ELIZABETH.
FLOTSAM & JETSAM.
SHIP SOCIETY OF SOUTH AFRICA, CAPE TOWN.
THE ARGUS (CAPE ARGUS).
THE TIMES, LONDON.
THE LONDON ILLUSTRATED NEWS.
THE GRAPHIC, LONDON.
COUNTRY LIFE, LONDON.
THE YORKSHIRE POST, LEEDS.
THE V & A. JOURNAL, CAPE TOWN.
SEA BREEZES.
SHIPS MONTHLY.
SHIPPING TODAY AND YESTERDAY.

ARCHIVE MATERIAL AND PHOTOGRAPHS .

MARITIME MUSEUM, GREENWICH.
MARITIME MUSEUM, CAPE TOWN.
THE SOUTH AFRICAN LIBRARY, CAPE TOWN
THE CHESTER LIBRARY.
THE ROLAND T. JACQUES UNION - CASTLE COLLECTION
THE PETER ABBOTT UNION - CASTLE COLLECTION

INDEX OF SHIPS

( ) illustration

OTHER PUBLICATIONS AVAILABLE FROM AVID.

LUSITANIA by Colin Simpson - updated Merseyside Edition

THE definitive work on the real story surrounding this still mysterious ship.

On the 7th of May 1915 the Cunard vessel Lusitania was torpedoed by a German submarine off the Old Head of Kinsale on the south west coast of Ireland resulting in the loss of the vessel itself and 1,201 men, women and children. It also ultimately resulted in the United States entry to the First World War. More than eighty years on the story of the Lusitania continues to be shrouded in mystery and suspicion. What was her real cargo? Why wasn't she protected? Why did she sink so quickly? Containing rare photographs from Germany and elsewhere; it is a truly intriguing and fascinating tale.

£9.50 + £1.50 p&p

LUSITANIA AND BEYOND-THE STORY OF CAPTAIN WILLIAM THOMAS TURNER
by Mitch Peeke & Kevin Walsh- Johnson. Illustrated by John Gray

There are many accounts of the great maritime disasters, but very few portraits of the people at the centre of these vast, tragic events. William Thomas Turner was captain of the RMS *Lusitania* when the giant liner was sunk by a German submarine attack in May 1915, with the loss of more than 1,200 passengers and crew. Turner survived, and this is his story.

A Merseyside man, he came from Victorian seafaring stock and his sole ambition was always to go to sea. Turner became the outstanding seaman of his time, who had learned his craft the hard way- by experience.

The loss of the *Lusitania*, bound for Liverpool from New York, shattered his world and over the years he has been accused of treachery, stubbornness, ignorance and much worse. This book gives the true, remarkable story of Captain William Thomas Turner, the last Master of the doomed *Lusitania*.

'...the Admiralty made 'thoroughly discreditable attempts to blame Turner for the loss'...'clears Captain Turner's name once and for all'...   Liverpool Echo

ISBN 0 902964 14 4   £7.99 + £1.25 p&p

ALL AT SEA - Memories of Maritime Merseyside
Compiled by Ev Draper. Foreword by Radio Merseyside's Linda McDermott
Introduction by David Roberts - Maritime Historian

A new book in conjunction with BBC Radio Merseyside's programme of the same name brings the voices of Merseyside seafarers and their lives to the printed page. Here are the stories of brave men, now pensioners, who survived horrendous incidents in the last two wars; stories of luxury liners, from Captains to cabin crew, of young lads forging their identity cards to get away to sea, and of their first eye-opening voyages.

ALL at SEA brings back the sounds and the smells of the docks, which remain vivid in so many people's minds, of busy tugs up and down the river, of men lost at sea; of women serving their country in different ways, and of those who provided guiding lights home. But through all the stories, there's one shining thread, the pride of Merseysiders in their seagoing traditions.

If you want real stories of the sea, told from the heart, by real people about real times and places, then this is a book for you. ISBN 1 902964 12 8   £5.99 + £1.25 p&p

JUST NUISANCE AB - His full story by Terence Sisson

The amazing but true story of the only dog that was officially enlisted into British Royal Navy, a Great Dane whose name was Nuisance, his official rank and name was AB Just Nuisance. Famed for his preference for the company of navy ratings (he wasn't too keen on Officers) in and around the famous World War II naval base of Simonstown, South Africa, Nuisance helped many a sailor rejoin his ship after a night on the town.

Today his own statue overlooking the bay off the Cape of Good Hope commemorates AB Just Nuisance.

£7.50 + £1.20 p&p

THE GOLDEN WRECK - THE TRAGEDY OF THE ROYAL CHARTER
by Alexander McKee

The effects great of the great hurricane of October 1859 were to shock the nation. 133 ships were sunk, 90 were badly damaged and almost 800 people lost their lives.

More than half of those that perished were on one ship - The *Royal Charter*.

The *Royal Charter* has a special place in maritime history as one of the greatest ever peacetime disasters. She was built at Sandycroft on the River Dee, the next-door neighbour to the river that was to become her home...the River Mersey. Soon after she was launched...sideways because of her great size for the day, she perhaps seemed ill starred in that whilst being towed down the river she grounded upon a sandbank off Flint, North Wales, and suffered serious damage to her main keel.

She eventually completed her maiden voyage to Melbourne in record time and her owners were able to boast about their new service 'England to Australia in under 60 days'.

Just a few short years later she was returning home and was hours away from disembarking her charges in Liverpool... until, when rounding Anglesey on the northern coast of Wales...disaster struck in the form of a Force 12 hurricane.

The people of the small village of Moelfre, Anglesey, came to the aid of the vessel and those from the ship who tried to escape the lashing waves and the deadly rocks. News of the wreck soon spread and the *Royal Charter's* other cargo, gold, became the focus of people's attention. Was all of it ever recovered? If not where did it go? The *Royal Charter's* gold still has the power to attract the adventurous and this book also explores attempts at salvage and treasure hunting more than 140 years on.

ISBN 1 9029640 2 0   £9.50 & 1.50 p&p

FORGOTTEN EMPRESS - THE TRAGEDY OF THE *EMPRESS OF IRELAND*
-by David Zeni

Tells the fascinating story of the Canadian Pacific Passenger liner *RMS Empress of Ireland*. On her way home to Liverpool from Canada, she was sunk in a collision on the St. Lawrence River. Two years after the *Titanic*, it was, in terms of passenger fatalities, an even greater tragedy. These two ships, along with the *Lusitania*, form a triumvirate of maritime tragedies, all within a three year period, that sent shock waves around the world.

Yet whilst *Titanic* and *Lusitania* seem to be almost household names, the disaster that befell the *Empress of Ireland* has until now always been shrouded in the cloak of history, as impenetrable as the fog that brought about her total loss, along with 1,012 lives, on 29th May 1914. With a chilling connection to the 'Crippen Murders' and containing never-before-published material, *Forgotten Empress* grips the reader in such a way it is hard to put aside... a thoroughly excellent book.

...dubbed 'The 'Forgotten Empress'...the second in a shocking trio of tragedies at sea...sandwiched in between the disasters of the Titanic *and the* Lusitania, *...it was a sudden death... that sent Liverpool into mourning...'*   Liverpool Echo

' Zeni brings a fresh, moment by moment urgency to this real life tragic drama."   Winnipeg Free Press

ISBN 1 902964 15 2 £10.50 + £2.00 p&p

CAMMELL LAIRD - THE GOLDEN YEARS
by David Roberts.

Looks back at the world famous shipyard's history with particular focus upon the 1960s and 70s when Lairds were engaged in the building of Polaris Nuclear submarines. A unique look at the history of this yard that contains many photographs and references.

'Captures life in the prosperous years of the historic Birkenhead shipyard' - Liverpool Echo
'Puts into perspective...the strikes...the Polaris contract...and those who worked at the yard' - Sea Breezes. ISBN 09521020 2 1   £5.99 + £0.80 p&p

LIFE AT LAIRDS - MEMORIES OF WORKING SHIPYARD MEN
by David Roberts

When Cammell Lairds has gone and we are a generation or two down the line who will answer the questions 'What did they do there?' 'What was it like?' This book answers the questions. - Sea Breezes
A Piece of Social History - Liverpool Echo

Life at Lairds is a book of more than 120 pages about what life was like for the thousands of ordinary people that worked in the world famous Birkenhead shipyard. Contains many rare photographs of Lairds, its' ships and its' surroundings. ISBN 0 9521020 1 3 £6.99 + £1.50 p&p

FASTER THAN THE WIND - A HISTORY GUIDE TO THE LIVERPOOL TO HOLYHEAD TELEGRAPH.
by Frank Large

Take a journey along the one of most spectacular coastlines in Britain, the beautiful hills and countryside of North Wales and Wirral. On a clear day it is possible to see just how signals were sent along the coast to and from Liverpool. This book contains full details of the intriguing and little known sites of the substantial remains of the Liverpool to Holyhead Telegraph Stations. A second journey can then be taken into the fascinating workings of such a telegraph and those people involved in creating and using the signalling system and what life was really like living and working at the telegraph stations more than 100 years ago. ISBN 0 9521020 9 9   £8.95 + £1.50 p&p

IRON CLIPPER – *'TAYLEUR'* – THE WHITE STAR LINE'S 'FIRST TITANIC'
by H.F. Starkey

'Iron Clipper' is subtitled 'The First Titanic' for it tells the story of the first White Star liner to be lost on her maiden voyage. Built on the Upper Mersey at Warrington, the *'Tayleur'* tragedy of 1854 and the *'Titanic'* catastrophe of 1912 are disasters which have so much in common that the many coincidences make this factual book appear to be a work which is stranger than fiction.

ISBN 1 902964 00 4   £7.50+ £1.40 p&p

SCHOONER PORT - TWO CENTURIES OF UPPER MERSEY SAIL
by H.F. Starkey

Schooner Port tells the story of the part Runcorn and navigation of the upper Mersey played in the Industrial Revolution and of the contribution of merchants, the shipbuilders, and the crews in making Britain 'The Workshop of the World'. Also recounted is something of the courage and tragedy, which was the lot of many flatmen and seamen who helped build British industry on the strength of the shipping fleet.

'Recognised as the only authoritative work on this particular subject' - Sea Breezes
'Packed with hard facts and illustrated with some rare old photographs, this rare book should command a wide readership'. - Liverpool Echo
ISBN 0 9521020 5 6   £8.95 + £1.50 p&p

FROM BATTLEFIELD TO BLIGHTY
The History of Frodsham Military Hospital 1915-1919 by Arthur R Smith

The horrors of the first 'Great War' are well known, but the stories of those sent back from the 'Battlefield to Blighty' tend to be overlooked. This is the little known story of one of the largest auxiliary military hospitals in the country that was established at Frodsham in Cheshire during the First World War.

Not for these men the modern diagnosis of Post Traumatic Stress Disorder or Stress Counselling after their ordeal... simply the green fields and fresh air of Cheshire and lots of TLC.

Over the period of the hostilities more than 3,000 patients were cared for at Frodsham Auxiliary Military Hospital and using a recently discovered set of contemporary photographs, '*From Battlefield to Blighty*' tells the stories of the doctors, the nurses, the patients and the local people who were involved in the Auxiliary Military Hospital at Frodsham. ISBN 1 902964 16 0   £7.99 +1.50 p&p

A WELCOME IN THE HILLSIDES?
- The Merseyside and North Wales Experience of Evacuation 1939-1945 by Jill Wallis

In the first week of September 1939 some 130,000 people left Merseyside for the safety of North Wales during World War II. Many were young children who had never been away from home before. Some didn't know why they were going, most didn't know where they were going. As they peered through train windows at unfamiliar hills and rolling countryside some youngsters thought they'd entered 'indian territory'; hearing a foreign language, others imagined they were 'in Germany'! Actually they had arrived in Wales.

A Welcome in the Hillsides? is an account of the Merseyside/NorthWales experience of the Second World War evacuation scheme. As hundreds of thousands poured into north and mid-Wales how did the authorities cope? - and how did the evacuees fare?

To produce a carefully balanced history the author has made an extensive search of official records and has also spoken to many of those who were involved in the scheme - former billeting officers, teachers, host families and, of course, the evacuees themselves! What emerges is an intensely human story - sometimes hilarious, sometimes painfully sad.   ISBN 1 902964 13 6   £9.95 + £1.90 p&p

VIDEOS
CAMMELL LAIRD - OLD SHIPS AND HARDSHIPS - the story of a shipyard.

After an extensive search for moving footage of this world famous shipyard at work a video of the history of this shipyard has at last been compiled. How Cammell Laird served the nation through two World Wars, building world famous vessels like the *Rodney, Hood, Mauritania, Ark Royal, Windsor Castle* and many more, up to the tragic day in 1993 when Lairds was shut down.

The story of the yard is also told through the voices of the men who worked at Lairds; Welders, cranedrivers, electricians and plumbers, they tell of the hardships of building ships in all weathers and the lighter moments that came from some of the 'characters' of the yard.

'ALL IN A DAY'S WORK.' Volumes I & II - - a look at working lives on the River Mersey.

Just when you might have thought that the River Mersey was dead and buried the biggest surprise of all comes along. There is life in the old dog yet! The River Mersey is alive and well. Liverpool, Birkenhead, Tranmere, Eastham and Runcorn are still places that enjoy marine traffic and employ people working on the river. There are interviews with River Pilots, shipbuilders, shiprepairers, tugmen and dredgermen that show that the age-old crafts and seamanship itself are still as strong as they ever were. There is also archive footage of working life on the river. Features Rock Boats, Mersey Ferries, the Bunker boats & crews on the Mersey, the Vessel Tracking System for river traffic, new vessels on the river, lockmasters and much more.   All videos are priced at £14.99 including post and packaging in UK.

Videos are also available in nternational formats price £17.99 + p&p £3.50.

144